Swan Dive Backwards

Swan Dive Backwards

FROM AI CURIOUS TO AI LITERATE

Susan Diaz

ISBN: 978-1-7387426-5-3 (Audio)
ISBN: 978-1-7387426-4-6 (e-book)
ISBN: 978-1-7387426-3-9 (Paperback)

For my dad.

You've been gone since 2014 and I think about what your face would look like watching me do this. Watching me become a two-time author. Watching me build something out of curiosity and stubbornness and a refusal to quit.

You would have had opinions about AI. Strong ones. And I would've loved to hear them!

I wish you were here so I could watch you watch me.

This one's yours, Appa.

Table of Contents

Chapter 1 Swan Dive Backwards ······ **1**
I Was NOT in the First Six Million ······ 1
An Ode to Sorting ······ 4
The Assessment That Rewired My Brain ······ 6
A Note on Belonging ······ 7
The Four Cliff Archetypes of AI ······ 8
Archetype One: The Divers ······ *9*
Archetype Two: The Pathfinders ······ *10*
Archetype Three: The Operators ······ *10*
Archetype Four: The Bridge Builders ······ *11*
Which One Are You? ······ 12
The Five Moves of a Swan Dive ······ 13
Move One: Spot the Cliff ······ *13*
Move Two: Check the Water ······ *13*
Move Three: The Actual Swan Dive ······ *14*
Move Four: Surface With a Map ······ *15*
Move Five: Build the Bridge ······ *15*
"A Few Moments Later" (Said in That TikTok Trend Way) ······ 16

Chapter 2 The Experiment Era ······ **18**
The Experiment-Only Trap ······ 19
The Blanket Ban Lie ······ 19

A Strategist Gets Stuck 20
The Parallel Universes 22
The "Unauthorized Site" Era (Again) 23
The Super Agent Myth 24
What Workflows Actually Mean (For Normal Humans) 24
Real Workflows, Real Problems, Real AI 26
The Hidden Costs of Experiment-Only AI 27
Hidden Cost #1: Duplicate Spend 27
Hidden Cost #2: Brand Drift 28
Hidden Cost #3: Risk and Compliance Exposure 28
Hidden Cost #4: Wasted Efficiency 29
Experimentation Is Good. Invisibility Is Expensive. 29
What to Do: Lead the Shift From Shadow to Structured 30
Step 1: Use the Leader's Script 30
Step 2: Create Simple Guardrails (Not a 40-Page Policy) 30
Step 3: Get Enterprise-Level Tools (Not Just Personal Subscriptions) 31
Step 4: Document Workflows, Then Build Playbooks 31
Step 5: Invest in Literacy, Not Just Licenses 32
Step 6: Leaders Go First 33
Who Owns This? (Spoiler: Not Just IT) 33
The Fear Underneath It All 34

Chapter 3 The AI Literacy Divide 36
The Jedi Council in your Office 37
The Biggest Sign you Have a Problem 38
A Tale of Two Workers 39
Watch What Happens in Meetings 40
The Divide Is Sharpest Where you Least
Expect It 41
Ditch the One-Tool Trap 42
The Comfortable Excuses 43
The Fear Nobody Talks About 44
Company A vs. Company B 44

What you're Actually Missing ········ 46
Setting the Baseline ········ 47
Two Things to Stop Doing Immediately ········ 48

Chapter 4 Leading the Archetypes ········ 50
Same Cliff. Different Wiring. ········ 51
The Leadership Playbook: Type by Type ········ 51
Leading Bridge Builders ········ 56
The Balance Check (a.k.a. Why your Team Feels Stuck) ········ 58
Where Each Type Fits in the Work ········ 58
The Cliff to Bridge Sequence ········ 60
Two Ways to Screw This Up ········ 60
Fix the Recognition (or Watch the Culture Break) ········ 61
Your Move: The Leadership Archetype Audit ········ 62
From Cliff to Crossing ········ 64

Chapter 5 The Audit ········ 65
Flying Blind Is Not a Strategy ········ 65
The 'Tools Feel Tangible' Trap ········ 66
The Tone That Makes or Breaks Your Audit ········ 67
A Framework - The 4 Dimensions of an AI Audit ········ 68
How to Run an AI Audit Without Boiling the Ocean ········ 69
Step 1: Listen ········ 69
Step 2: Map the Tools ········ 70
Step 3: Document Workflows ········ 71
Step 4: Map Adoption Patterns ········ 73
Step 5: Assess Risk and Governance Gaps ········ 73
Step 6: Highlight Opportunities ········ 74
The Costs of Skipping the Audit ········ 74
The Audit Output That Doesn't Die in a Folder ········ 75
Audit as the Middle of a Bigger Journey ········ 76
Your Move: The 60-Minute Audit Starter ········ 77

Chapter 6 Training · · · 79
The Monday Morning Test · · · 80
Why One-Off Training Fails · · · 81
The Login Trap · · · 82
You're Teaching a Language, Not a Feature Set · · · 83
The Readiness Gate (Check Before you Train) · · · 84
Framework: The 4 Layers of Sticky Literacy · · · 85
Build the Editor Mindset · · · 89
Building Training That Actually Changes Monday · · · 90
Step 1: Define the Outcome · · · 90
The Personal Aha (Why Home Use Matters) · · · 92
Your Move: The Monday Morning Training Brief · · · 93

Chapter 7 The AI Flywheel · · · 95
Projects End. Flywheels Compound. · · · 96
The Moonshot Trap · · · 97
Framework: The 4 Pillars of the AI Flywheel · · · 98
Pillar 1: Audit (The Reality Check) · · · 98
Pillar 2: Training (Building the Floor) · · · 99
Pillar 3: Personalized Tools (Workflow First, Tool Second) · · · 100
The sequence that matters: · · · 102
Pillar 4: ROI (The Story That Keeps the Wheel Funded) · · · 102
Metrics That Actually Matter · · · 103
The ROI of 'Good Enough' · · · 104
Culture: The Ring Around the Flywheel · · · 105
The Compounding Advantage · · · 107
How to Start the Wheel · · · 108
Your Move: Your First Centimetre · · · 109
The Wheel Doesn't Need a Documentary · · · 110

Chapter 8 Culture as the OS · · · 112
AI Adoption Is a Human System · · · 113
Why the Experiment Era Makes Culture Visible · · · 114
What Culture Actually Means in an AI Context · · · 115

Framework: The Culture OS (6 Pillars) 117
Pillar 1: Playgrounds and Guardrails 117
Pillar 2: Psychological Safety 118
Pillar 3: Transparency as a Default 120
The 'No AI' Policy Problem 120
Pillar 4: Quality, Voice, and Accountability 121
Bad Tools Create Security Risks 122
Pillar 5: Access and Inclusion 123
Pillar 6: Mentorship That Scales 124
Different Learners, Different Needs 125
The Power of Community 125
Three Patterns That Sabotage Adoption 128
Design a Purposeful AI Culture 129
Culture Wraps Around the Flywheel 130

Chapter 9 Buy / Build / Bolt-On 131
RPA for the Mind 132
The Queen Bee Strategy 133
The First Rule: Map the Workflow Before You Touch the Tools 133
The Unsexy List (Your Most Powerful AI Tool) 134
The Three Options Framework 135
Option 1: Buy 135
Option 2: Bolt-On 136
Option 3: Build 136
The Six Levels of Personalized Tools 137
What Building Actually Looks Like (in the Wild) 138
Dr. Jim's Approach: Role, Task, Output 139
The Chain Rule 140
Automation Versus Autopilot 141
Decision Filters That Actually Work 142
Your Move - the Circle Exercise 144
The Decision Sentence 144
The Real Goal is White Space 145

Chapter 10 Building Your Beehive ···· **147**
What a beehive actually looks like (not the metaphor, the reality) ···· 148
Pick your workhorse first ···· 149
Train it like a team member ···· 150
The 'feed it everything' rule ···· 151
The builder thread: using AI to build your AI ···· 152
The No-Build Alternative (or: what if you just talked to it?) ···· 153
When your context is the product ···· 158
The sprawl problem (or: when your hive gets overrun) ···· 159
The visibility fix ···· 161
What this looks like at scale ···· 162
Your move: build your first bee in thirty minutes ···· 164
Step 1: Name the micro-task ···· 164
Step 2: Write the Role, Task, Output ···· 164
Step 3: Add three guardrails ···· 165
Step 4: Test with three real examples ···· 165
Step 5: Write one sentence that defines success ···· 165
The point of building is not output. It's white space. ···· 166

Chapter 11 AI Champions ···· **168**
What's actually happening (whether you designed it or not) ···· 169
Champions are a bridge. ···· 170
The unpaid help desk problem (and why it ruins everything) ···· 171
The first skill is finding them ···· 172
The audit question that finds champions ···· 172
Don't fall into the loudest voice trap ···· 173
The 10pm experimenters ···· 174
The imposter trap ···· 175
The Three R's of champion support ···· 176
Recognition: name the role ···· 177
Resourcing: give time and support ···· 177
Repositories: turn personal hacks into shared assets ···· 178
Champions should be guides, not gatekeepers ···· 179

The Champion Blueprint 180
Connected champions beat lonely champions 181
What the support system should actually look like 182
Your move: the one conversation 183

Chapter 12 Does AI make you more or less creative? 184
Paintbrush vs. Photocopier 186
AI Creates Options. Humans Create Meaning. 187
Creativity is how organizations stay distinct. 188
The Driver's Wheel 188
What to Do: Five Ways to Use AI Like a Paintbrush 189
AI Doesn't Do Courage 191
The Mirror 192

Chapter 13 ROI Beyond Time Saved 193
Why "Hours Saved" Keeps Failing You 194
Build the Stack, Not the Slide 196
Metric 1: Quality Lift *196*
Metric 2: Risk Reduction *197*
Metric 3: Speed to Opportunity *198*
Metric 4: Decision Velocity *199*
Metric 5: Learning Velocity *200*
Building the Dashboard: Three Layers 201
The Invisible ROI: First-Order vs. Second-Order Benefits 202
Measuring "Stuck Work" (A Simple Method) 203

Chapter 14 The AI Gender Gap Nobody's Closing Fast Enough 205
The 25% Gap 206
It's Systemic. Not Personal. 206
The Job Displacement Danger Nobody Wants to Name 208
The Flip: Why This Moment Is Also MASSIVE Opportunity 209
Heather's Vision (And Why It Matters) 210
Mini Exercise: The Permission Slip 211
The Call to Organizations 212

Chapter 15 35,000 Reasons for Hope ······ **214**
The Number Nobody's Talking About ······ 215
The Milk Delivery Man ······ 215
We Have Literally Done This Before ······ 217
The "Purple Person" and the Jobs That Didn't Exist ······ 218
The Real Headline: It's a Hop, Not a Cliff ······ 219
The Upskill or Lay Off Question ······ 220
What the Real Goal Actually Is ······ 221
Mini Exercise: The Hop Map ······ 223

Chapter 16 The Swan Dive ······ **225**
The 30-Day Dare ······ 225
The Name ······ 226
The Messy Middle ······ 227
How AI Actually Built This Book ······ 228
The Five Moves, One More Time ······ 230

What I Want You to Take With You ······ **232**
The Voices in This Book ······ 234
Voices Behind This Book ······ 241

CHAPTER 1

Swan Dive Backwards

"I swan dive backwards off the cliff into AI."

I've said this enough times that it's basically my catchphrase now.

And every single time, people laugh. Then they pause. Then they lean forward. Because the phrasing sticks.

If you picked this book up, either because it called out to you or because you're a long-term listener of my podcast and you followed along on the 30-day podcast-to-book sprint, THANK YOU! This is the moment you find out how the whole dang thing came to be. So buckle up. Let's talk about cliffs and commitment and what it actually looks like to move when there is no path ahead of us.

I Was NOT in the First Six Million

Let's rewind to the end of 2022.

ChatGPT drops. OpenAI releases this thing into the wild and suddenly there's a stat floating around: six million people signed up in the first WEEKEND.

Six. Million. People.

In a weekend.

That goes beyond adoption into stampede territory.

And me? I was not in that stampede.

I sat it out. I watched from the sidelines. I'm not a Luddite. Neither do I hate new things. That said, I've been a marketer for a REALLY long time. Like, my entire adult life, basically.

And over that time, especially in the seven-ish years before 2022, I'd seen a parade of "AI tools" march through my workflows. Text-to-video converters. Transcription software. Pattern spotters. Headline generators.

Some of them were fine. Most of them were underwhelming.

Clunky interfaces. Limited functionality. Output that was juuuust good enough to make you think it might save time, but then you'd spend SO much time fixing it that you'd end up just doing it yourself anyway.

So when people started buzzing about ChatGPT, I wasn't swept away. I wasn't cynical, either. I was just... not organizing my entire life around it.

This was not my first AI rodeo, folx.

Then, about a week later (call it Weekend Two), a couple of friends whose judgment I trust sent me messages that were variations of *"Are you on this thing?"*

And I was like, okay. OKAY. If these specific humans are losing their minds over it, I should probably check it out.

So I did.

And within about five minutes, I could feel it. Something had shifted.

I couldn't NAME it yet. But I could feel it in my body before I could articulate it in my brain.

Now, after a few years of speaking engagements, classrooms, workshops and explaining this to THOUSANDS of people, I can tell you EXACTLY what that shift was.

It hit a trifecta. Three things that hadn't existed together before in the average AI tool for the masses:

> **Credibility.** The output wasn't perfect (and we've all seen the jokes about people posting AI content with wildly hallucinated "facts" in it), but it was credible ENOUGH. Like, 60 to 80% depending on who's driving. Which means you never have to start with a blank page again.
>
> **Power.** It could handle LARGE volumes of information. Not just a sentence here or a headline there. We're talking full documents. Messy brain dumps. Voice notes that ramble. Mind maps that don't make sense yet. It could take all of that and do something useful with it. FOR YOU.
>
> **Access.** It was free. FREE. Credibility plus power plus zero dollars is a lustworthy combination we didn't know we always wanted.

By coming to market with that combo, OpenAI forced everyone else to speed up their AI game. And gave rise to an arms race style approach that has all the big tech spewing updates and features like their bills are being paid by a Sugar Daddy.

The winners in all of this? Us. The people. The users.

So no. I wasn't in the first six million.

But when I showed up on Weekend Two, I became the person who was late to the party and then completely refused to leave. *(You know that person. The one who arrives at 9pm and is still there at 2am helping clean up? Yeah. That's me.)*

An Ode to Sorting

We'll get to the good stuff in a minute. But first, let's talk about sorting. Humans LOVE to be sorted.

Think about it. From the time you were a little kid, sorting was everywhere. You were sorted into classes. Into teams for dodgeball. Into reading groups that everyone knew were ranked even though the teachers pretended they weren't. Into 'houses' sorted by colour at the school I went to in Chennai, India.

And then along came a woman named J.K. Rowling who created the most culturally sticky sorting mechanism of our generation. *(Sucks rotten eggs that she turned out to be a trans-hating bigot which I will not endorse, but the Harry Potter series endures.)* My grandma bought me Harry Potter books in my late twenties. She read them in her seventies and knew it would appeal to my whimsy.

The Sorting Hat.

Gryffindor. Slytherin. Ravenclaw. Hufflepuff.

I'm Gryffindor, all the way. *(Obvi.)*

And here's the thing. When you got sorted into your house, either by the official Pottermore quiz or just by vibes, something HAPPENED in your chest. You felt it. You were like, "*YES. That's me. That's my people.*"

Why?

Because sorting, done well, is an act of love.

It's someone *(or something - hey, Sorting Hat. I'm still not quite sure if you're someone or something)* looking at you and saying: **I see you**. I see how you're built. I see what drives you. And there's a place for you here.

That's why we identify so deeply with these things. That's why the Enneagram girlies will fight you to the death over their number. That's why people used to put their Myers-Briggs type in their resumes. That's why, if you've ever done DISC or StrengthsFinder or the Fascination Advantage assessment, you remember your result YEARS later.

Because for a moment, you felt seen.

Now. I've come across A LOT of these frameworks in my career. Some of them were built for more niche audiences by brilliant women entrepreneurs who introduced them to me. Coaches and consultants and facilitators who used sorting as a way to help their clients understand themselves. And every time, I walked away understanding something new about how I tick.

This chapter (and this book) is an homage to all of them. To the women who built businesses around the deeply important work of helping other humans figure out who they are. To the idea that understanding yourself is not a soft skill. It's a STRATEGIC one.

And I want to bring that energy into how we think about AI adoption.

The Assessment That Rewired My Brain

Years ago, when I was running my digital marketing agency, I had a client who was DEEPLY into Kolbe. If you're not familiar, it's an assessment methodology that measures how you naturally take action. It was their love language. Every team member had done it. Every meeting referenced it. They spoke in its vocabulary the way some families speak in movie quotes.

And they asked me to do one. To help them understand how I was wired, so we could work together better.

I'll be honest. I'd done plenty of personality assessments before. Myers-Briggs. Others. They were interesting. Some were helpful. But none of them had ever really cracked open something I didn't already know.

So I agreed for a lark and from a place of always being open to learning. Especially about myself.

The Kolbe assessment showed me that I was long in what they call "Quick Start". Which is the part of you that thrives on jumping into new things, taking initiative, embracing uncertainty. Yep. Checks out. Tell me something I don't know.

But here's where it got interesting. I was ALSO long in "Fact Finder". Which is the part of you that needs to research, analyze, and understand before acting.

And when I saw those two things sitting next to each other, something clicked. For years, YEARS, people had told me I was "high risk". Like it was a character flaw. Like the fact that I moved fast and made big bets and started businesses and threw myself into new things was somehow reckless. Irresponsible. Something to be managed or apologized for.

But looking at those results, I realized: I'm NOT reckless. I never was.

I take CALCULATED risks. I research the hellz out of something and THEN I jump. The jump looks impulsive to people who only see the jump. They don't see the fact-finding that happened at 2am the night before.

That reframe explained fifteen years of entrepreneurship. It explained every crazy decision I'd ever made that somehow worked out. It explained why I swan dive backwards. I'm not closing my eyes and hoping for the best. I'm scanning the water, checking for rocks, and THEN committing fully.

A Note on Belonging

Before I introduce you to the four archetypes (yes, we're getting there, I promise), I need to say something about why sorting matters so much in the context of AI adoption specifically.

Belonging.

As co-host of the ABCDEI podcast, I've spent a lot of time in the diversity, equity, and inclusion space. And one of the things that comes up again and again in that work is this: when people don't see themselves represented in a system, they disengage. Because the system wasn't built with them in mind.

We're seeing this play out with AI RIGHT NOW. If we look at the leadership of this technology, you might think it is built for a certain type of person. Young. Male. Technical. Silicon Valley coded.

And that's garbage.

I'm a proponent of women being given space to develop AI-forward skills. Not as a nice-to-have diversity initiative. As a wage gap closing imperative. As an economic necessity. As a matter of basic equity.

So when I sort people into archetypes in this book, I want you to understand where that impulse comes from. It comes from the same place as the Sorting Hat. From the same place as every brilliant woman who ever handed me an assessment and said, *"Let me help you understand yourself."*

It comes from love. From the belief that when people see themselves in a system, they lean in. They participate. They stop standing at the edge thinking *"this isn't for me"* and they start moving.

And EVERYONE deserves to see themselves in the AI conversation.

The Four Cliff Archetypes of AI

Okay. So. What does swan diving backwards actually look like in an organization? What does it look like to recognize you're at the edge of a cliff, decide not to freeze, and then jump with your eyes open in a way that's actually USEFUL for yourself AND other people?

Inside any company, you'll have people who think in all four of the ways I'm about to describe. Some in permutations and combinations you never dreamed of.

You've got Divers and Pathfinders and Operators and Bridge Builders.

That's what inclusive AI adoption looks like.

Enter the **Four Cliff Archetypes of AI Framework**.

Let's break it down. And as you read these, pay attention to where you feel that little PING. That *"oh, that's me"* moment. Because just like the Sorting Hat, the goal is to show you where you naturally shine so you can lean into it.

So let me paint you a picture.

Imagine four people hiking up a mountain. Same trail. Same pace. Same destination. Everything's fine.

Then they all arrive at the same point where the trail just... disappears.

No warning. No detour sign. Just a sheer drop down the side of a cliff.

Now watch what happens.

Archetype One: The Divers

These are my people. These are the divers.

We look over the edge and we're like, *"Oh. Well. I guess we're going down."*

And we take a leap of faith.

This is not mindless. This is not a suicide mission. We do a quick scan. We check for rocks. We make sure there's water. We tuck our elbows in. We do the thing.

But the default move is to MOVE. Not to freeze.

In your company, these might be the people who are quietly experimenting with AI for content strategy, research, automations, workflow stuff. And they're doing it BEFORE anyone told them it was allowed.

(Because why would you wait for permission to solve a problem?)

Archetype Two: The Pathfinders

These folx show up to the same cliff and they're like, *"Hang on. HANG ON."*

How deep is this thing? Is there another route that's safer? Can we form a human chain? What happens if we break our legs? Do we have a plan for broken legs?

These are the plotters. The strategists. The researchers. The people who sketch routes and think through scenarios and make sure we don't all die.

And we LOVE them. Without them, we'd all be dead. They're keeping us from splattering our brains on the rocks.

Archetype Three: The Operators

Once the route is agreed on, these folx step up.

They're the doers. The action takers. The ones who put the little signs in, tie the ropes, organize the people, make sure the actual process of going down is SAFE. Oh, and they're the ones that will make the common stockpile of snacks from everyone who comes that way. Just in case!

You always need the people who can take a plan and execute it. Always.

(I used to call this crew executors. I'm not doing that anymore because that sounds like they're killing someone in a B-grade movie plot. So. Operators it is.)

They run pilots. They document what you learned. They integrate tools into other processes. They figure out how to make the change STICK. Because sometimes things come in hot and everyone's all hyped up and then two weeks later it's like... what were we talking about again?

The Operators make sure that doesn't happen. You'll find these folx in operations (duh), project management, implementation roles. They're the ones making theory into reality.

Archetype Four: The Bridge Builders

And then there's this fourth group.

These are the systems people. The infrastructure thinkers. My husband is in this group, by the way, so I recognize them deeply.

These are the folx who look at the whole situation and say, *"Okay. Now that we know what we know, let's build a BRIDGE."*

They're not interested in one-time solutions. They're thinking about the next person who comes to this exact spot on the trail. That person shouldn't have to make the same decision we did.

They're building Centers of Excellence. Governance frameworks. Ongoing support. They're impressed by INFRASTRUCTURE, not heroics.

And this matters because a true swan dive backwards is not about how brave the Diver was.

It's about getting to a point where nobody else has to dive.

Build something that LASTS.

Which One Are You?

You probably already know. You felt the ping.

The important part is that there is no wrong answer. This isn't a ranking. The Diver is not better than the Pathfinder. The Operator is not lesser than the Bridge Builder. Every archetype is essential. Every one of them has a role in making AI adoption actually work.

What matters is that you KNOW which one you are. Because when you know your natural wiring, you can stop fighting it and start using it. You can stop apologizing for the way you move through the world and start leveraging it.

Want to find your archetype? I've built a quiz that will help you figure out which of the four cliff archetypes is your lead. You'll also get access to all the mini exercises from this book, bonus resources, and some additional frameworks that didn't quite make it into these pages but are too good not to share.

Scan the QR code below or visit: https://wearenorthlightai.com/swan-dive-backwards

Now let's talk about the process that connects all four archetypes together.

The Five Moves of a Swan Dive

If the Four Archetypes are the PEOPLE, this next framework is the PROCESS.

Because a swan dive backwards is a pattern. Like all good machine learning. And once you see the pattern, you can repeat it. You can teach it. You can use it as a leadership method.

Welcome to the ***Five Moves***!

Move One: Spot the Cliff

A swan dive starts when you realize we're not on an incremental path anymore. The path ENDED. For me, that was the moment I realized this generative AI thing wasn't just another tool. It wasn't another software update. It was a milestone technology. The kind that changes what normal work looks like.

Like the calculator. Like the personal computer. Like the internet.

For enterprises, the goal is to stop saying, *"We'll look at AI later"* and start saying, *"We need to change the way we work RIGHT NOW."*

Move Two: Check the Water

Divers don't jump onto rocks.

This is the guardrail step. The governance step. For me, this looked like running a LOT of tests. What is AI good at? What does it suck at? I did everything from cleaning email lists to building complex custom tools that now run entire sections of my business.

I ran enough tests that some of them FAILED. And when they failed, I learned what doesn't work. I learned how to question the output. I learned how to amplify what's working.

Organizationally, this is where governance lives. What data is safe to use? What data is NEVER allowed? Where are the gray zones? How do you ask for help? What does human review actually mean in practice?

Governance is what makes speed SAFE.

And here's a crucial note for leaders: you can't delegate this entirely. You can partner with experts. You can rely on Pathfinders. But you can't outsource the UNDERSTANDING. If you don't personally use AI for your own work, you won't be able to sponsor it well for your team. You'll be leading from theory. And that's a shaky place to stand when the path has disappeared.

Move Three: The Actual Swan Dive

This is the jump. This is where you decide not to stay in analysis paralysis. This is where you accept that you're going to be a beginner, but you start anyway.

You start using it on REAL work. Not simulated toy environments. Not sanitized examples. Not cute little demos that never exist in the real world.

Real work is messy. It has contradictions and context and office politics. It has partial information and implied meaning. THAT'S where AI either becomes useful or reveals its limits.

For leaders, this means personally using AI for your own stuff. And if you're already doing that, expand it. Make it workflow-based. String multiple things together. Sponsor experiments for your teams. Signal that it's okay to try, to learn, to adjust.

This is where you move from theory into practice.

Move Four: Surface With a Map

This is where organizations fail quietly.

They dive. They experiment. They move on. And the learning stays in someone's head. The wins remain private. The organization never gets smarter.

Surfacing with a map means taking what happened in the dive and turning it into something SHAREABLE. Documentation. Language. Patterns. A workflow that can be repeated. A list of risks that can be mitigated. A rubric for "good enough".

Bring back a map of your lived experience.

Move Five: Build the Bridge

This is the part that makes the title worth keeping. A swan dive backwards is not a permanent operating model. It's a transitional move. It's what you do when the trail disappears and you have to choose movement over freezing.

The goal is not to keep diving forever. The goal is to build a BRIDGE. Infrastructure. Training that holds. Tools that fit workflows. Governance that guides instead of terrifies. Metrics that tell the truth. Culture that keeps the learning visible.

That's what this book is ultimately here for. Not bravery. Not hype. Not a thousand isolated experiments.

Infrastructure.

"A Few Moments Later" (Said in That TikTok Trend Way)

It was the end of 2025 when I recorded the 25 podcast episodes that gave me the raw material for this book. At this point I'd been posting about AI for several years. I've mentioned this whole swan-dive-backwards thing on a few podcast episodes, both my own and some that I guested.

Several people asked me, *"Are you writing a book?"*

Enough times that I noticed.

I still don't really crystallize in my brain what seems quite obvious as I'm writing this. Hindsight really IS 20/20!

So eventually I take this 30-day challenge. Huge shout out to Dan Sanchez and Ken Freire. They took on this project and shared their process with a great deal of transparency and generosity. They invited anyone who'd like to join the challenge. Not sure anyone else was crazy enough to accept. I was. I had this book in my head and I wanted to get it out before we started a new cycle of time.

So I record daily episodes of the podcast for a month, and decide to use THOSE to write this book.

(Because of course I'm using AI to help write a book about AI. It would be ridiculous if I didn't.)

I write a post about this challenge on LinkedIn. And something very cool happens.

A name pops up in my comments. Someone who's been a friend for MANY moons. (Or maybe many SUNS, given the amount of time that's passed.) Her name is Alison Garwood-Jones. She was one of my professors when I did my Digital Marketing Strategy certificate at the University of Toronto.

She writes this comment: *"I really hope you get this book done. And I really hope you call it Swan Dive Backwards. I'll leave the subtitle to you."*

And when I read that, something just... landed.

LANDED.

This was it. The book had a name. The energy was right. The story was baked into the title. MAYBE it landed for you too because it made you lean forward and pick up this book.

So now you know the backstory. And here's the core idea I want you to walk away with no matter how far you choose to read into this book.

You can choose to move boldly into AI. You can choose to do it BEFORE the path is fully built. That is the heart of this book.

CHAPTER 2

The Experiment Era

The hidden cost of experiment-only AI.

Think about the last really inspiring conference you went to.

You know the kind. The speakers were GOOD. The energy was high. You took notes like your life depended on it. You left buzzing. Your brain was FULL. You felt smarter just walking to the subway station (or Ubering to the airport, depending on how fancy your company is).

Then real life hits.

Two weeks later, you're staring at your scattered notes trying to remember what the hell mattered. You know it felt important. You know there was something you were supposed to DO with all this. But you can't remember what. (And if you're being honest, maybe you're not even sure where you put the notebook.)

That feeling? That's where a LOT of organizations are with AI right now.

There's activity. There's energy. People are playing with AI models, testing ideas, trying different tools in the cracks of their day. But almost

NONE of it is structured. Almost none of it is visible to leadership in a way that turns "cool" into "compounding".

Activity is not the same as progress, folx.

Experimentation is great, but the invisibility of your experiments is a problem.

The Experiment-Only Trap

The Experiment Era has a particular flavor.

It FEELS innovative from the inside. It LOOKS chaotic from the outside. And to leadership? It often looks like nothing is happening at all.

Because the real work is happening in private prompts, personal accounts, and unshared documents.

When experimentation stays invisible, it can't compound. A win happens in a silo. No one else learns. The organization never benefits.

That's the quiet cost that never shows up on a line item. It's not the software fees. It's the OPPORTUNITY COST. The creative energy that should be building momentum but never becomes a system.

The Blanket Ban Lie

Let's put a gentle truth on the table.

(Gentle notwithstanding, I know this is going to sting a little.)

Even if your organization has a blanket "No AI" policy currently, people are not following it.

Not because they're villains. Not because they don't respect the rules. But because they're busy, intelligent, and surrounded by utility. They can FEEL the difference between "what would help me right now" and "what I'm allowed to use".

And in the modern workplace, the answer to a hard problem often exists on a literal device in their pocket.

So while Legal is writing Draft 5.0 of the AI policy, people are already using ChatGPT. Or Claude. Or Gemini. Or whatever tool gives them the result they need with less friction. *(And honestly? Most of them are paying for it themselves. Twenty-five bucks a month. The cost of a fancy set of pens. Why WOULDN'T they?)*

If you're leading as if bans create compliance, you're leading a fantasy. The organization is living reality.

A Strategist Gets Stuck

Here's a scene that's playing out in offices RIGHT NOW.

A strategist is building a deck. Or wrestling an Excel sheet into something that resembles a story. They hit a block. The kind of block that makes you stare at the screen and think, "Why is this so HARD? We have AI. What am I missing?"

So they open the approved internal assistant. The safe one. The one blessed by IT and governance and good intentions. They type in their questions.

The answer comes back.

And it's... fine.

Safe. Generic. Missing nuance. Missing the micro-specifics of the market, the internal politics, the constraints that actually shape decisions.

It's the AI equivalent of getting directions from someone who's never been to your neighborhood. Technically correct. Practically useless. Because it misses all the real directions you need, like "turn left at the alley behind the stunted maple tree near the house with a thousand wind chimes."

(You know EXACTLY which house I mean.)

And THAT'S the moment the Experiment Era reveals itself.

Because the strategist KNOWS the answer exists elsewhere. They know it will take ten minutes to solve with a more capable tool. They also know they're not supposed to use it.

So what happens?

They do what smart people do.

They strip out the names. Remove the obvious identifiers. Take out the details that feel incriminating. Then they open their personal account (on their phone, or a personal laptop), and they get the job done.

That's how shadow AI happens.

Not from malice. From friction.

The Parallel Universes

Most organizations now have TWO AI universes running at the same time.

Leadership sees one. Work happens in BOTH.

Universe One: The Official Universe
Approved enterprise tools

Safer (but often limited)

Visible to leadership

Documented

"Allowed"

Universe Two: The Unofficial Universe
Personal, highly capable tools

Lives on private devices

Where the real work happens

Outside your guardrails

Beyond your visibility

The Official Universe is what you THINK is happening. The Unofficial Universe is where problems get solved quickly. And here's what makes this sticky: you can't block utility. People will ALWAYS find a way to do their jobs better. It's hardcoded in all of us.

The "Unauthorized Site" Era (Again)

If you're old enough to remember this, you're about to feel VERY seen.

(If you're too young to remember this, bless you.)

Fifteen years ago, many organizations were still blocking the use of work internet for anything other than a few approved sites. *(Heck, I'd guess there are still a few companies that do that in 2026)*. You'd click a link and BAM. Pop-up message: UNAUTHORIZED SITE.

Like you were trying to access porn instead of, you know, Googling "Excel formula count unique entries with multiple conditions not working."

(Which, for the record, was EXACTLY the kind of thing we were Googling. Or Yahoo-ing. Remember Yahoo? Good times.)

People worked around it. They used their phones. They posted in forums. They found YouTube tutorials *(much, much, MUCH later)*. They figured it out.

We are REPEATING that pattern right now.

If someone can't get what they need inside the organization's knowledge base, they WILL find it. They've always found it. AI is simply the new path of least resistance.

There's no reason to panic. We do have to stop pretending bans are strategies though.

The Super Agent Myth

The Experiment Era also creates a particular kind of fantasy. People want ONE super agent. One magical entity that replaces entire departments. One automation that eliminates complexity. One tool to rule them all. *(Yes, I went full Lord of the Rings there. Not sorry.)*

I understand the desire. Complexity is EXHAUSTING. But this is where leadership needs to get clear-headed.

AI can absolutely replace STEPS. It can draft first versions. It can clean data. It can summarize and collate information. It can generate alternatives and scenarios.

What it CANNOT reliably do is replace an entire PROCESS that requires social comprehension, ethical judgment, relational nuance, and decisions rooted in values.

Stop chasing the super agent. Start documenting the process.

The real opportunity here is to change the doom and gloom narrative from "humans are going to be replaced" to this: "humans will be ELEVATED".

Compress timelines. Reduce drudgery. Increase impact. Up-level the type of work your people are doing. That's the game. The infinite game.

What Workflows Actually Mean (For Normal Humans)

I know some of you just read "workflow" and your brain went fuzzy. Let me make this SUPER simple. A workflow is just the steps you take to get something done. That's it. It's not fancy. It's not technical. It's just: what do you do first, second, third to turn raw material into finished output?

Here's **Jason Dea**, a product leader who's been working in SaaS and startups for years, breaking it down: *"Don't think about the tools you're using. Just literally think about the 10 steps in a granular way.*

Step one: I open an email box.

Step two: I see what's in the email box.

Step three: I find the thing that I'm looking for.

Step four: the thing I'm looking for has an attachment."

Those steps? THAT'S a workflow.

AI is not a magic wand that'll fix your entire workflow in one shot. It's an enabling technology that lets you rethink SPECIFIC parts of your workflow. The parts that are boring. The parts that are repetitive. The parts that make you want to throw your laptop out the window.

Jason uses this metaphor that I LOVE: *"think of AI as a swarm of bumblebees".*

You're the queen of the hive. You have jobs that need to get done. Some you don't want to delegate or outsource. But others? They're difficult, time-consuming, highly repetitive, or just plain boring. So you build a team of little worker bees. Each one does a SPECIFIC task. And together, they create this hive of efficiency.

Not one super bee. A swarm of little specialized bees.

That's how you should be thinking about AI.

(BTW: There's an adorbs story behind this metaphor. Jason's kid was studying bees for science in elementary school. And talking about bees made this metaphor stick for Jason as a leader in the start up world. LOVE that.)

Real Workflows, Real Problems, Real AI

Let me give you a real example from Jason's world. He works with enterprises in legacy industries like financial services and insurance. And you know what the backbone of those industries still is?

Paperwork.

Specifically, SCANNED paperwork. Like, literal photos of pieces of paper.

(I know. I KNOW. But it's true.)

Historically, scanned documents have been really difficult to work with. OCR (optical character recognition) technology has been around forever, but it was predicated on tight rules. If somebody's handwriting went outside the box on a form? The machine got confused.

But that's actually an IDEAL use case for AI. Because generative AI excels at what Jason calls *"gray area decision making"*. It can look at messy handwriting, context clues, and partial information and still figure out what's going on.

So if you map out the workflow (receive document, scan document, extract data, enter data, validate data, file document), you can spot the friction point. The place where humans are doing repetitive, annoying work that a machine could handle better? THAT'S where you inject AI.

And suddenly, you've removed the toil from the workflow. You've freed up humans to do the things machines CAN'T do, like making judgment calls based on ethics, relationships, and company values.

The Hidden Costs of Experiment-Only AI

The Experiment Era is messy and it's EXPENSIVE. Not in the obvious way. Not as a single line item you can blame on someone. It shows up as scattered costs, diluted quality, and missed leverage. Here are the big ones:

Hidden Cost #1: Duplicate Spend

Without a strategy, Marketing buys a writing tool. Sales buys a campaign tool. Ops buys a summary tool. HR buys something else for internal comms.

Often these tools OVERLAP. Sometimes wildly.

You end up paying for similar capabilities five or six times across departments, with no unified view and no leverage at renewal time. (And then Finance looks at the P&L and is like, *"Why are we spending THIS MUCH on AI tools?"* And nobody has a good answer.)

Shona Boyd, a product manager in SaaS who's been working to make AI more approachable, put it this way: *"It's very important to understand the difference between enterprise-level security and just regular 'I purchased this myself' security. There IS a difference when we're looking at different LLMs."*

When everyone's buying their own subscriptions with their own credit cards (or worse still, using free versions with no security), you lose visibility. You lose control. And you definitely lose negotiating power.

Hidden Cost #2: Brand Drift

Brand has always been a hub-and-spoke model. Even when execution is distributed, there is a central point of control. A brand guide. A voice. A person who said "no, that's not how we sound".

Experiment-only AI breaks that without anyone noticing.

When everyone generates content in their own private AI silos, the voice dilutes. Messaging becomes inconsistent. The brand starts to sound like a generic LLM. Small shifts compound. And eventually, the company feels less like ITSELF.

Hidden Cost #3: Risk and Compliance Exposure

Shadow AI is a major RISK.

People paste sensitive data into public models. Confidential documents get uploaded. Internal context leaks. Sometimes without anyone even realizing what they've done.

You increase exposure to privacy violations, regulatory breaches, loss of intellectual property, and reputational risk.

Shona Boyd has seen this firsthand: *"I used to work at a law firm, so I am very much not about that life. But a lot of people are like, 'Oh, I'll just use my own personal ChatGPT.' You just downloaded a table of data with metrics and uploaded it to your personal one. Oh gosh."*

What's particularly scary here is that leadership often doesn't know WHERE this is already happening. (If anything, they're thinking this would never happen in their company.)

Hidden Cost #4: Wasted Efficiency

Sometimes experiments work. Someone finds a faster way. They quietly keep using it. It makes their job easier.

Great, right?

Except it stays trapped in their HEAD.

The team doesn't learn. The department doesn't standardize. The organization doesn't benefit. What could have been shared leverage becomes lost in a ChatGPT thread of a previous employee.

Experimentation Is Good. Invisibility Is Expensive.

I want to be VERY clear about this: Experimentation is a sign of a curious culture. You WANT people who look at new capability and ask, *"How can I use this to make my work better?"* That's initiative. That's innovation. That's people firing on all cylinders.

The leadership question is NOT *"How do we stop experimentation?"*

The question is: **How do we encourage experimentation WITH guardrails, and make the learning visible?**

Because if experiment-only is your operating mode (no visibility, no shared learning, no measurement), that's expensive. In money. In risk. In opportunity.

What to Do: Lead the Shift From Shadow to Structured

Leaders can start by acknowledging reality, then building safe structure around what is ALREADY happening.

Step 1: Use the Leader's Script

Don't punish. Don't pretend. Name reality out loud.

Say something like this: *"I know many of you are already using AI tools. You're using our internal ones, and you're using your own. I want to understand what you're doing so we can support you. Let's make this safe and strategic."*

That sentence CHANGES THE ROOM. It turns secrecy into collaboration. It tells people you're not here to shame them. You're here to build a system.

Step 2: Create Simple Guardrails (Not a 40-Page Policy)

You don't need a 40-page compliance document yet. (Honestly, if you have a 40-page compliance document, nobody's reading it anyway.) You need a ONE-PAGE "rules of the road".

Simple Guardrails (One Page)
What's OK to put in public tools?

What must NEVER leave the organization?

How do you ask for help or escalate concerns?

This is the BEGINNING of safety. Shona Boyd's advice here is gold: *"We need to have conversations, especially in organizations that have private and protected information. We need to understand. And we need to make it open so people don't have to sneak and do it because that is such a breach of privacy."*

Step 3: Get Enterprise-Level Tools (Not Just Personal Subscriptions)

This is where a lot of organizations mess up. Especially the smaller businesses. They let people use their own subscriptions. Or they hand out logins without understanding the difference between consumer-grade AI and enterprise-grade AI.

Here's what Shona recommends: *"I would probably pick the workhorse, like a ChatGPT or a Claude depending on your usage. And I would set that up at the enterprise level because that allows you to actually use your data and connect it to your internal data points, which makes the answers it gives you SO much better. It's looking at your drives, your data, your metrics in your organization. And that information STAYS THERE. It does not go out there somewhere. It stays in your instance."*

That's the difference. Consumer tools learn from your inputs. Enterprise tools keep your data locked down.

Step 4: Document Workflows, Then Build Playbooks

The word "playbook" is used SO BADLY in business. (It's right up there with "synergy" and "circle back" on my list of words that have lost all meaning.)

A playbook is a book of PLAYS. In a sports context, it's a collection of specific moves you execute in specific situations. In an AI context, that means DOCUMENTED WORKFLOWS. If you don't have the workflows, you don't have a playbook. You have a wish list.

Start small. Pick a handful of high-repetition workflows. Document them. Spot the patterns. Create shared assets people can use and improve.

Documentation is how experiments become infrastructure.

Step 5: Invest in Literacy, Not Just Licenses

This is where leaders get seduced. Buying licenses feels like progress. It's visible. It's easy to approve. You can point to it in a meeting and say, "Look! We're doing AI!"

But literacy is what makes tools USABLE.

Tools without training mean nothing. Licenses without literacy is just playing dress-up.

Shona breaks down what literacy actually means: *"It's really about critical thinking, not necessarily understanding specific frameworks, but understanding how to talk to an LLM. And being able to critically think through the outputs it's giving you and being able to look at your individual workflows and pick workflows that could really benefit from the use of AI."*

If you want sustainable adoption, invest in the HUMAN ability to use the machine well (safely, critically, and consistently). My company, Northlight, does exactly this. If you don't know how to build AI literacy at scale, we should chat. Connect with me on LinkedIn. Use this QR Code for LinkedIn.

Step 6: Leaders Go First

Here's Jason Dea's advice for leaders, and it's critical: *"The best way to get past the hype of AI and get closer to the tangible benefits is to really try it yourself. Incorporate it into your day-to-day. Even the busiest executives (or actually ESPECIALLY the busiest executives), their days are probably full of toil. See if you can incorporate AI in an effective way into your own workflow. If nothing else, it should give you context as to how granular you should be breaking down that task to really achieve the benefit. And then you can speak in a more grounded way when it comes to implementing AI into your corporate strategy."*

You can't lead what you don't understand. And you can't sponsor what you don't use. If you're not personally using AI for your own work everyday, you'll be leading from theory. And that's a shaky place to stand when the path has disappeared.

Who Owns This? (Spoiler: Not Just IT)

One of the most common mistakes I see is organizations defaulting to IT to "own" AI.

And I get it. It's technology. IT handles technology. The math checks out, right?

Wrong.

Shona Boyd's take on this is spot-on: *"IT, of course, has the licenses to make sure everything is up to par and locked down. But it really needs to come from leadership. When it's at the department level, you start seeing weird one-off cases that may not be locked down. You can get better use of your budget if you have certain licenses at a top level. And you avoid creating haves and have-nots between departments."*

Jason Dea echoes this: *"AI fundamentally is about workflows and tasks. And more specifically, it's about the democratization of being able to deliver on those things. IT has an important role when it comes to governance. But the old-school model where IT had to both govern AND implement? That's changing. AI is empowering end users to do things they couldn't do before."*

So who SHOULD own it?

Leadership sponsors it. IT governs it. Departments implement it. And everyone learns together.

The Fear Underneath It All

Let's talk about the thing nobody wants to say out loud in real life circumstances. People are SCARED. They're scared AI will replace them. They're scared if they get too good at using it, they'll teach the machine how to do their job. They're scared that if they admit they don't know how to use it, they'll look incompetent.

And leaders? Leaders are scared too. They're scared of falling behind. They're scared of making the wrong bet. They're scared of the board asking, "What's our AI strategy?" and not having a good answer.

Fear is never really fear of the THING. It's fear of CHANGE.

And change management is HARD.

Shona Boyd's advice here is beautiful: *"I think it's really important that we keep that empathetic framework and empathetic view around how people are feeling in this day and age. We hired you for your mind and for what you're bringing to the table. Use AI to make your work go a little quicker, to analyze things a little faster. But we still need the human in the loop."*

That's the message leaders need to be sending.

AI is here to ELEVATE you not replace you.

CHAPTER 3

The AI Literacy Divide

Many organizations have an AI literacy problem. And I don't mean literacy in the "can you log into ChatGPT and type something" sense. I mean literacy the way the financial industry talks about financial literacy. Or the way the health sector talks about health literacy.

Think about it.

Financial literacy means you understand what interest is. You know how debt works. You get why compounding matters. Health literacy means you understand what a fever is. You know when to see a doctor. You understand why prevention beats emergency care.

AI literacy is the same deal. It's a baseline understanding that everyone needs. Not just the tech folx. Not just IT. Not just the curious few who are running pilots and sharing cliff notes.

EVERYONE.

And right now? That's not how most organizations are operating. What they have instead is an AI literacy divide. Some people are curious. Some are getting fluent. They're moving fast with their experimentation.

Others are avoiding the topic entirely. Or they're flash-in-the-pan users because someone mentioned a tool at the virtual water cooler.

Meanwhile, leadership is trying to make decisions in the dark.

And THAT is why AI adoption stalls.

The Jedi Council in your Office

I'm a visual thinker. *(And a Star Wars nerd, obvi.)* So let me paint you a picture. Imagine a council meeting. Everyone's sitting around a table trying to make a big decision about AI.

On one side, you've got the Yoda-led faction. These are the calm, deep-thinking, long-view people. They already sense with the Force that AI is a shift. They GET that this is like when the interwebs became a thing and everyone suddenly needed a website. Or when social media exploded. Or when everyone optimized for mobile.

Except this time? It's more exponential. And the shift is happening in a shorter window.

Within that pro-AI group, you might also have some overly optimistic types. Too fast. Too many tools. Convinced there's an AI answer to everything but nothing major is actually getting documented or improved.

On the other side of the table, you have the folx reading the doom and gloom headlines. They're talking about job losses. Deepfakes. That time a lawyer submitted case law that didn't exist. *(Hallucination 101, not the end of the world with the right checks and balances. Which this situation lacked.)*

I'm not saying these aren't valid concerns. There are ALWAYS valid concerns when major technological shifts happen. But we have the tools to minimize the risks. To de-risk it as best we can.

And then there's the third group. The silent middle. These folx don't say much. They're not loudly pro-AI. They're not loudly anti-AI. They're just waiting for someone else to figure it out and tell them what it means for their role.

That's what AI literacy looks like in a lot of companies right now.

The Biggest Sign you Have a Problem

If your leadership team has never truly sat down to talk about AI as a cultural, strategic, and operational shift, that's the biggest sign you may have a problem.

Things might be starting from the bottom up. And that's okay.

But the THINKING needs to come from the top.

Has your leadership sat down? Do they sit down regularly at this stage? What's the learning plan?

And I'm not talking about vendor pitches where people with tool arrangements are teaching you something. I'm not talking about a few slides being presented by someone who tried a few prompts.

When I say REAL conversation at a leadership level, I mean articulating a vision. How does this organization plan to take on this AI transformation era? How do we make it safe to talk about fears and risks? How do we map out what this could look like short term, medium term, long term?

Because, remember, experiments are already happening whether or not it's approved.

When that conversation hasn't happened, what you get is teams and individuals jumping in at different levels. Often it's chaotic. Unstructured. Undocumented. People are learning the same things over and over again.

There's no shared language.

That's what a literacy divide looks like. It starts with not having a clear vision.

A Tale of Two Workers

Let's make up a fable. Inside your organization, there are two people. One is a confident AI experimenter. The other feels quietly left behind.

Person One? They jump into new tools without waiting. If your CRM has an AI component, they're already in there figuring out what to do with it. Anytime they're looking at a complex problem, they're thinking, *"There has to be a better way."* And the better way usually involves AI.

They're using AI to summarize. To draft. To reframe. To explore and research things before starting from a blank page. They're not spending time learning about all the tools. They're using the tools so they can spend more time on judgment and action.

Person Two just doesn't feel strong in their AI knowledge. So their week looks REALLY different. They're doing things manually the way things have always been done. They're spending time teaching themselves things from scratch that AI could have accelerated. Maybe they're avoiding it because they're afraid of doing something wrong.

And over time, these two paths compound.

Person One frees up capacity. Takes on higher-level work. Thinks more strategically.

Person Two? Doesn't.

Same organization. Same tools available.

But unless you have a clear vision for what AI literacy looks like, and you bring people with you on that vision, and you execute at every level, this divide is going to compound.

Watch What Happens in Meetings

Meetings are a quick diagnostic. Pretty much every meeting in every organization has some mention of AI. Even if you have an enterprise-wide ban on AI tools currently, there are still mentions of it.

Spend some time observing. You won't be able to unsee the patterns that I'm laying out in our fable!

Some people speak up. These are probably your early adopters. They see AI as a milestone development, just like with early internet and digital transformation. They're moving the conversation from hype to systems. *"How can we use it for our business? How does this work? Who can we talk to?"*

Others bring up worst-case scenarios.

And then there's a whole lot of people who say nothing. Because they're not sure if they're in a safe place to admit that they don't know (or don't care).

The first thing to do is make it safe enough for people to say, *"Hey, I don't know. What's the plan?"* Then you ask, *"How would you like to learn?"* Then you put that together.

The Divide Is Sharpest Where you Least Expect It

The literacy divide is often the sharpest at the leadership and middle management level. The executives and middle managers are often a little bit behind the more junior folx.

Why?

Because many of the grassroots-level employees (at desk jobs) are jumping in feet first. There's zero way their work ISN'T getting better because of it. They're comfortable experimenting in their own time.

But leadership and middle management? They're usually too busy. Learning new tools makes them feel like a beginner again. Maybe they're self-conscious about not knowing enough. Maybe it's awkward to be the manager of someone who knows way more about AI than you do.

So you end up with this weird dynamic. The people with the formal power are not the ones with the most lived experience with AI. And the people with lower amounts of power are getting there quickly.

How do you spread it around?

Ditch the One-Tool Trap

If you're in a place where you're dabbling with AI but it's not really moving the needle, most often the problem is that you're too focused on finding one super agent or one tool. *"Is there ONE tool that can help me do this?"*

No, folx. It's not even possible at a department level. It's not even possible at a sub-department level. It's not even possible in an organization of ten people.

You're going to need multiple things. And THAT'S why the literacy thing needs to sink in.

Let the penny drop.

Stop thinking about a one-size-fits-all solution. Stop thinking about AI like it's one platform you have to learn, like a CRM. It's more like the internet. It runs through everything. There isn't one magical chatbot that everyone will suddenly use. The LLMs are the closest thing to that, but inside organizations, there are guardrails. Or there should be.

That's why you need to look beyond the tools. Look into the unglamorous work.

Map out how things are currently done without AI. It can look as simple as boxes and arrows and lettering on a whiteboard. Find the friction points. Where is it hard? What do you not want to do? What do you not want changing hands six times? What do you want to cut from six steps to four?

THAT'S where AI can help you.

The Comfortable Excuses

Sometimes enterprises get into comfortable excuses that slow down adoption even further.

"Compliance needs to sign off on this."

"We need to wait for more mature solutions."

"Our business needs something specific."

Are there governance concerns? Absolutely. But sometimes these excuses are just a cover. A way to pause. Delay. Avoid. Because a big change is underway. And avoidance feels safer than action. But uneven literacy is going to be a bigger issue than we realize. Because it goes beyond just a few people being more effective and a few people not.

You're going to have haves and have-nots inside the same organization.

The have-nots will feel threatened, sidelined, resentful.

The haves, because they're doing things faster, will end up having to do MORE work. And feel resentful too.

See where this is going?

I'm painting a bleak picture. I realize that.

But in order to establish an honest baseline, it's important to unpack this. And I don't know that a lot of people are going to unpack this for you.

The Fear Nobody Talks About

I mentioned fear in the last chapter. Let's unpack that some more. Underneath all of the AI talk (the tools, the tactics, the hype), there are human beings. And what people are afraid to say out loud in many cases is this: *Is my job going to change? Is my role going to disappear?*

Yes, I understand that future roles will emerge. But are those two things going to line up?

It's hard.

And paradoxically, the less honestly you talk about these fears, the more likely it is that the worst-case scenario actually happens.

If most organizations are just telling their people, *"No, there's gonna be no job losses"*, I'm not sure that's accurate. At some point, there will be some. Maybe you don't need people who perform a pure research function or a pure writing function anymore. Then what happens to the writers and researchers? Will they get a different job? Will you train them from today so that when things shift in two years, they actually have something?

If you say nothing... If you don't plan... If you don't retrain and redesign those jobs, then people are going to get left behind.

Company A vs. Company B

Let me paint you another picture. Two companies in the future.

Company A:
Experimentation is happening in some pockets. Some mapping out is happening. But there's no clear shared documentation of all your workflows.

Training exists in one-off webinars and vendor-led stuff. The curious people are teaching themselves in isolation. The cautious people are firmly on the sidelines.

Leadership is hearing "AI is amazing and saving us hours!" from one department. And "It's risky, we shouldn't be touching it" from another.

No single source of truth. No coherent strategy. No measurable progress.

Company B:
There's a baseline literacy across the organization. Not mastery yet, but enough so that people can work together.

Leadership has held regular conversations about AI. They've painted a vision. Put timelines into place. They've made it safe to talk about fears.

They've run an audit to see if AI is already in use and where. What are the risks?

There are workshops across departments. Internal staff. Experts talking to your people. Not just demos from tools, but real sessions to surface strengths and fears and current workflows.

There are documented processes. They know where AI is helping. They know where it shouldn't be used. There are quality standards for what good looks like.

There's a strong knowledge base. Maybe a system of buddy groups pairing people to experiment. Maybe some type of brain trust or a community internally for people to learn. Maybe you're bringing in facilitation as needed.

And they're regularly up-leveling. Compounding. They're not done, but they're on the path.

The difference is intentionality.

Which company do you want to be?

What you're Actually Missing

If you stay in the "we're all feeling in the dark and trying to figure this out" mode, you're not just missing productivity gains. People are still getting things done, right? What you're missing is INNOVATION.

This is an incredible moment in history. AI can take a huge chunk of everyday drudgery off our plates. That frees up time and headspace for people to live in their true genius.

(The concept of "zone of genius" is from ***Gay Hendricks in his book 'The Big Leap'****. That's the kind of work only you can do. At the risk of sounding woo-woo, it's what you came here to the earth to do.)*

AI can help people stay in that zone. And by extension, it can help organizations tackle the big, hairy problems that really matter.

Maybe we can end world hunger. Take away the concept of poverty. Create peace.

There are HUGE possibilities.

But if AI literacy stays uneven, some people are going to stay trapped in low-value, repetitive work. The same patterns of bias and exclusion are going to get repeated.

Setting the Baseline

So let's set that baseline. Let's think beyond a couple of webinars. A couple of internal brainstorming sessions. Let's put in place the concepts and practices and feedback loops.

What does a baseline AI-literate organization actually look like?

Everyone can explain in plain language what LLMs can do and what they can't. They understand that these are pattern-matching systems, not magic brains.

They know how to spot and fix issues. How to use a basic set of prompts to get the output they need. How to map at least one of their own workflows and sync it to a department level.

They know how to evaluate what they get and say, *"This is not good enough, let's go deeper".*

THAT'S the stuff every single person in the organization needs to know. That's when you have a floor. A starting point.

From there, you can build specialized skills. Custom tools. Advanced workflows.

And it's going to get exponential.

Two Things to Stop Doing Immediately

As we wrap this chapter up, I want you to think about two things. Or rather, two things I want you to STOP doing at once.

Stop treating AI as a binary.
It's not. There's no "we are for AI" and "we are against AI". It's not like you missed a fork in the road and it's over.

If you're thinking, "This shouldn't be here, this isn't great for humankind", the moment to stop it would have been several decades ago. Not now. It's already here.

You're at a point in history where you have a calculator on your desk. If you choose to turn it upside down and say, "I'm not going to use it because I don't think it's right", and... I mean... you've played it out. You know how that goes. Everyone has a calculator in their palm in the form of a mobile device. And that's what's happening with AI.

It's not a binary. You're not for it or against it. It's a matter of HOW you're going to get there and setting that vision.

Stop pretending there are no inequities in this process.
Don't reinforce existing inequities. As you build out AI literacy, don't make it "only leadership gets this" or "only designed for tech folx".

And here's one a lot of people won't say out loud: don't let it only reach mostly men because they're the ones who step up to the plate for tech! We need to collectively make a much deeper effort than that.

Don't leave out certain demographic groups because they're not the ones stepping up.

Because if that gets by on your watch, you're baking that inequity deeper. AI already comes with a lot of bias baked in. The reason it has bias is because it learns from human interactions. And humans are intrinsically biased.

CHAPTER 4

Leading the Archetypes

Divers. Pathfinders. Operators. Bridge Builders.

You met these four in Chapter 1. You saw them standing at the edge of the cliff. You watched them react. Now let's talk about what happens AFTER the introductions are over and you actually have to lead them.

Frameworks are fun to learn. They're satisfying to name. And then Monday morning rolls around and your diver has gone rogue with a new tool, your pathfinder has requested a third round of research time before approving anything, your operator is building a dashboard for a workflow nobody validated yet, and your bridge builder is writing a policy document based on exactly zero real experiments.

(Ask me how I know.)

Spotting and naming the archetypes aren't the hard part. LEADING them is.

Same Cliff. Different Wiring.

Some AI initiatives feel strangely easy. They catch traction. People try things. Value shows up quickly. Other initiatives feel like you're dragging a couch up a staircase. Same organization. Same budget. Same access to tools. But somehow, nothing sticks.

It's not the tools. It's not even the training. *(We covered the literacy gap in Chapter 3)*

It's the SEQUENCING of your people.

If you've got all divers driving an initiative, you'll get speed and shadow AI and a pile of experiments nobody can reproduce. If you've got all pathfinders steering the ship, you'll have immaculate risk logs and nothing shipped. If operators are running it solo, you might get a beautiful machine pointed at the wrong target. And if bridge builders are leading before there's anything real to standardize, you'll get governance documents that gather dust.

(I said it nicer in Chapter 1. I'm being blunter now because we're four chapters in and you can handle it.)

Your archetype isn't your identity. It's your default response under uncertainty. And the leadership move is NOT to turn everyone into the same type. It's to sequence the work so each type shines at the right moment.

The Leadership Playbook: Type by Type

In Chapter 1 I gave you the quick version of each archetype. Here's the more textured version intended to help you LEAD them. Complete with the shadow sides I glossed over. *(Because Chapter 1 was about getting you excited. Chapter 4 is about getting you effective.)*

Leading Divers

The sentence you'll hear: *"Let me just try this."*

I'm a diver. I told you that. So believe me when I say this next part comes from a place of deep personal experience.

Divers are gold for adoption. They generate velocity. They find use cases faster than committees can schedule meetings. They show what's possible. They create the raw material your organization can later refine into workflows and standards.

They are also the reason your IT department has a migraine.

Because divers move fast. They don't always document. The steps are clear in their head, so writing it down feels slow and unnecessary. They may not pause long enough to consider what data they just fed into a public tool. And without meaning to, they can set an expectation that everyone should move at diver speed.

(Which, for the record, most people can't. And shouldn't.)

When diver energy is running the room without guardrails, you could get what we talked about in Chapter 2. Tools in use that leadership doesn't know about. Outputs no one can reproduce. Small risks accumulating quietly. A growing gap between the folx who are playing and the folx who are watching.

The leadership task is NOT to shut divers down. Give them a sandbox instead of a straitjacket.

Your diver playbook

Create safe zones for experimentation AND clear boundaries for what's off limits. Specific data, specific IP, specific do-not-cross lines. Then get out of their way.

Build a channel for sharing experiments. Weekly or biweekly. Short, informal, low-stakes. The goal is to make the experiments VISIBLE so the organization benefits from the speed.

Reward two things divers don't naturally prioritize: documentation and teaching. When divers share what they tried and what they learned, the whole team gets smarter. When they don't, you've got a brilliant person carrying knowledge in their head. Which is the opposite of scaling.

And this one is HUGE: protect your divers from becoming the unofficial AI help desk. Nothing burns out a diver faster than being the person everyone pings with *'hey can you show me how to do this thing'.* They need time and space to keep experimenting. If you turn them into tech support, you'll lose the very energy that makes them valuable.

Remember: divers don't typically create shadow AI because they're hiding. They create it because they're moving. If nobody has offered a safe place to test, they'll create their own.

Leading Pathfinders

The sentence you'll hear: *"Whoa, hold on. Where does this lead?"*

Pathfinders hit the cliff and immediately scan the terrain. They want to understand what's hiding: risks, privacy issues, compliance gaps, dependencies, and downstream consequences you haven't even thought of.

You'll hear it in the questions. *Where's the evidence? What's the use case? What's the downside? Do we have a policy for this?*

Pathfinders can be frustrating to people who want speed. But they are often the reason companies avoid disasters. They prevent dumb mistakes. They reduce drama. They spot the quiet risks that become loud incidents later.

(We LOVE the pathfinders. I said it in Chapter 1 and I'll say it again.)

The shadow side is just as predictable: pathfinders can get trapped in permanent evaluation. One more round of research. One more validation cycle. One more committee review. AI moves FAST. And pathfinders can turn caution into avoidance without realizing it.

When pathfinder energy is leading the room without time-boxes, you get analysis paralysis. Momentum slows. Divers grow impatient and go underground. Operators start implementing whatever they can because the organization feels stuck. Bridge builders try to standardize too early because nobody is providing stable inputs.

Your pathfinder playbook

Honour their value first. These folx need to know that their scanning is respected, not tolerated. If they feel like the team sees them as blockers, they'll either dig in harder or go quiet. Neither helps you.

Then give their caution a cadence. Two-week sprints work well: Research, Recommendation, Next Experiment. It's less about rushing and more about preventing 'more research' from becoming the default comfort zone.

A simple tool here is the one-page memo. Ask for three things: *What do we know? What don't we know? What should we test next?* That structure gives pathfinders control without letting the project stall. It also turns their scanning into a usable asset the whole team can reference, not just a vibe in the room.

Trust pathfinders with risk mapping and governance design. That's where they SHINE. Then make sure that risk mapping converts into movement.

Leading Operators

The sentence you'll hear: "*Tell me the plan.*"

Operators are less interested in philosophical debate and instead want clarity. Goals. Roles. A definition of 'done'. The first step, the next step, who owns what, what the timeline is, and how success will be measured.

(These folx are the reason anything actually HAPPENS in your organization. Respect the energy.)

Operators take an initiative out of the messy idea-stage and turn it into actual execution. They build the machine. They run the machine. They keep the machine running. They're also the people most likely to save you from innovation theatre because they ask the blunt question: '*What are we actually doing here?*'

Operators also have a quiet risk. They can execute the wrong thing beautifully.

If leadership hands operators a tool-first mandate, 'Use AI', 'Roll out this platform', 'Automate X', without workflow understanding, operators will implement a shiny thing nobody uses. Because they're built to execute. And if what's been handed to them is vague, they'll make it concrete in ways that might not serve the actual goal.

Your operator playbook

Don't give operators AI. Give them TARGETS.

Translate AI into specific workflows: proposals, onboarding, customer service, reporting, whatever your business runs on. Then assign metrics operators can own. Cycle time. Error rate. Adoption rate. Time saved. Throughput. Operators need to know if they're winning. When success is measurable, operators will drive momentum all day long.

Without that clarity, they'll produce activity that looks like progress and feels like disappointment. They'll build dashboards for things nobody asked for. They'll run training on tools that don't fit workflows. They'll do ALL of it with excellence. And very little will matter.

Give operators templates, playbooks, SOPs. Ask them to help BUILD those things as they execute. They're natural at creating the 'how we do it here' documentation that bridge builders can later scale.

And this is key: make them share learnings as part of execution, not as an afterthought. If operators are only measured on output and never on insight, you miss half their value.

Leading Bridge Builders

The sentence you'll hear: *"No one should have to jump this every time."*

Bridge builders see the cliff and think about infrastructure. They want to make AI safe and repeatable for EVERYONE. They translate chaos into shared language. They turn messy experiments into documentation, playbooks, onboarding, and a culture of 'this is how we do it here'.

(My husband is a bridge builder. He's the reason our household has systems. I'm the reason our household has stories.)

Bridge builders love reuse. They want frameworks people can pick up and apply. They care about scaling: how do we make this consistent across teams, not just brilliant in one pocket?

Bridge builders are how you go from ad hoc activity to real organizational advantage. Full stop.

But they have a predictable risk: premature optimization. If bridge builders start building bridges before you've learned where the cliff really leads, you get policies nobody follows and training nobody remembers. Process without proof. Governance that isn't connected to lived reality.

Over-engineering is often a reaction to uncertainty. When the cliff feels scary, building rules feels comforting. It creates a sense of control. But bridges built too early tend to be built to the wrong place. You need to get clear on where the traffic is.

Your bridge builder playbook

Feed them the right raw material. Real experiments. Real workflows. Real friction points. Real examples of what 'good' looks like. Then ask them to standardize the top five workflows first. Not fifty. Five.

Pair them with divers. This is maybe the most powerful combo in the whole framework. Divers generate raw experiments. Bridge builders systematize them. Together they create momentum AND infrastructure.

Build guardrails intended to ENABLE, not restrict. And create shared assets and approved use cases so bridge builders can anchor their work in reality, not theory.

The thing to remember: bridge builders create leverage when they systematize what's ALREADY working. If they're systematizing ideas that haven't been tested, you're building a bridge to nowhere.

The Balance Check (a.k.a. Why your Team Feels Stuck)

Here's where this becomes immediately useful. You do NOT want a team full of any one type.

All divers? Chaos. Speed without safety.

All pathfinders? Paralysis. Governance without movement.

All operators? Impressive execution of possibly the wrong thing.

All bridge builders? Process without proof. Policy without traction.

You need a mix. Because it's the ONLY way to cross the AI cliff repeatedly without losing people or trust along the way.

And here's the biggest mistake leaders make: assuming their own archetype is the 'right' archetype. If you're a diver, you'll hire divers. If you're a pathfinder, you'll reward caution. It feels smooth. It also creates blind spots. And those blind spots become your bottlenecks.

Where Each Type Fits in the Work

Once you can see the archetypes, you can stop guessing where momentum is getting stuck.

To help you meet your people where they are at in the AI literacy journey, I've created a **quiz for 'The 4 AI Cliff Archetypes"**. You can find it, along with other bonus resources to help you implement AI, as well as all the mini exercises in this book. The link is wearenorthlightai.

com/swan-dive-backwards or scan the QR code below if you're using a printed copy of this book.

Now here's a simple map.

In auditing and discovery (figuring out where you are now): pathfinders lead. They ask the questions that prevent you from building on sand. Bridge builders support by capturing learning and organizing what's emerging. Divers help by surfacing what's already happening in the shadows, because divers tend to know where the unsanctioned experiments live.

In training (building the floor): bridge builders tend to lead. They're natural curriculum designers. They build standards. They create community. Operators support by making the rollout real: scheduling, attendance, accountability. Making sure enablement isn't just a slide deck that disappears. Divers bring the examples. Real prompts, real workflows, the *'here's what I tried'* stories that make training stick.

In custom tools and implementation (raising the ceiling): divers prototype quickly, operators implement with stability, pathfinders validate risk and fit, and bridge builders standardize so the organization can repeat the win.

In tracking ROI (proving it works): operators build dashboards and adoption metrics, bridge builders create reporting cadences, pathfinders sanity-check what you're measuring, and divers pressure-test with new cases so you don't overfit your system to yesterday's reality.

If your initiative feels jammed, look for what's MISSING in the room. That gap is almost always your bottleneck.

The Cliff to Bridge Sequence

This is the sequencing model that keeps momentum without sacrificing safety. Say it with me:

Divers jump. Generate experiments.

Pathfinders map. Validate risk and opportunity.

Operators ship. Turn what works into execution.

Bridge builders scale. Standardize so others can cross safely.

This sounds simple. It IS simple. It's also the difference between AI adoption as chaos and AI adoption as a repeatable organizational muscle.

The sequencing matters because it stops you from asking each archetype to do work they're not built for.

Two Ways to Screw This Up

Every framework has ways it is misunderstood. Here are the two I see most.

Failure Mode #1: Using archetypes as personality verdicts.
"She's a diver, so she's reckless." "He's a pathfinder, so he's a blocker."

That's lazy leadership wearing new vocabulary. The archetypes describe default responses to uncertainty. They're not moral categories. If you use them to judge people, you'll create resentment and you'll lose the benefit of the model.

Failure Mode #2: Pretending your team is balanced when it isn't.
Many leaders can name the archetypes and still keep staffing initiatives the same way they always have. Same handful of reliable people, regardless of fit. If you do that, the framework becomes a fun workshop and nothing changes. Balance is less philosophy and more sequencing decisions made quickly.

Fix the Recognition (or Watch the Culture Break)

If your recognition system is misaligned with the work, culture breaks. Before or after AI this is fact.

If your recognition system lacks, people start protecting themselves instead of building capability. Learning slows. Blame increases. And the whole initiative starts to feel like a chore instead of a mission. Here's how to match recognition to each archetype:

Reward divers for **documentation and teaching**, not only for clever experimentation. A diver who writes down what they tried and teaches someone else is worth TEN divers who experiment in silence.

Reward pathfinders for **enabling safe progress**, not for proving they found every possible problem. The goal isn't a complete list of risks. The goal is informed forward motion.

Reward operators for **outcomes**, not for activity. There is a huge difference between 'we ran training' and 'people changed how they work'. Measure the second one.

Reward bridge builders for **standardizing what works**, not for producing process volume. Five workflows that people actually follow beats fifty workflows nobody uses.

Your Move: The Leadership Archetype Audit

Alright, folx. Here's where you turn insight into action. Give yourself twenty minutes. Don't overthink it. *(Seriously. The pathfinders reading this are already planning to spend two hours! Twenty minutes. GO.)*

Step 1: Think of three or four key players/leaders you rely on to move major initiatives. Write their names down.

Step 2: Assign each a primary archetype, as best you can. You're allowed to guess. Use your best judgment based on behaviour, not job title.

Step 3: Ask two questions. Where are we overloaded? Where are we empty?

Overloaded might look like: too many divers and leadership trying to shut them down. Or too many pathfinders steering the conversation and nothing shipping.

Empty might look like: no bridge builders to standardize. No pathfinders to map risk. No operators to ship. No divers to prototype.

Step 4: Pick one active AI initiative. Map the archetypes to the work.

Who is generating experiments?

Who is mapping risks?

Who is shipping the workflow?

Who is standardizing and training?

If one of those boxes has no name, you just found your first bottleneck.

Step 5: Make ONE change this week. Not ten. One.

Pair a bridge builder with a diver. Time-box a pathfinder's research cycle. Give an operator a clear metric. Protect a diver from being turned into the help desk.

The point isn't perfection. The point is movement with intention.

This, and all the other mini exercises in this book are in one easy place for you to access. Scan the QR code below or visit: https://wearenorthlightai.com/swan-dive-backwards

From Cliff to Crossing

AI will keep feeling like a cliff because it keeps shifting what's possible. That's the nature of this moment. Your job isn't to eliminate the cliff. Your job is to build a team that knows how to cross it.

When you can name these behaviour patterns, you can design for them instead of fighting them. You stop treating AI like a cliff you fear and start treating it like a cliff your team knows how to navigate. Again and again. With growing confidence.

That's what archetypes give you. Not a label.

A map of human motion.

And one hell of a better leadership strategy.

CHAPTER 5

The Audit

How to stop making AI decisions on guesswork.

Let me ask you a question that's going to make some of you uncomfortable. Do you ACTUALLY have a full picture of what's happening with AI inside your organization right now?

Not what your vendor dashboard says. Not what your strategy deck suggests. Not what you hope your people are doing. Not the cute pilot you announced at the leadership offsite.

What is real. On the ground. Inside workflows. Right now.

If you hesitated even a little bit, this chapter is for you.

Flying Blind Is Not a Strategy

Many organizations are flying blind on AI. Because as we discussed in chapter 2, AI is already inside the building, and nobody has drawn the map of where it lives *(or even given it an office)*.

HR may be using resume filtering that runs on machine learning they forgot they bought in 2021. Operations has AI features baked into their ticketing tools and ERP systems. Marketing is testing copy and content workflows on three different platforms. Individual contributors are paying for personal ChatGPT subscriptions and using them to get through the day.

None of this shows up in a centralized dashboard. Much of it isn't documented. Some of it is completely invisible to leadership until something goes sideways.

Jennifer Hufnagel, whom you've met earlier in the book, is an AI readiness consultant who has trained 4,000+ people. And she says that companies come out with all these studies saying AI adoption is 83% or 90%. *"At the end of the day, I'm not sure who they're talking to, because they're not in the rooms that I'm in."* When Jennifer asks people whether they've used generative AI tools or created automations, the answer is usually no. The official adoption numbers and the reality on the ground are currently living in two different universes.

An audit is how you make the invisible visible. That visibility is the foundation for everything that follows: training, governance, workflow redesign, tool decisions, and an ROI story that your CFO will actually respect.

No audit. No baseline. No story.

The 'Tools Feel Tangible' Trap

Here's why leaders skip the audit. Tools feel tangible. A platform contract. A pilot. An internal GPT. An 'AI lead'. A training program. It all feels like movement. It makes for a clean announcement. It gives you the comforting sensation of 'we're doing something'.

But without an audit, you're guessing.

Jennifer sees this a lot: *"People are so focused on the tools. They're writing AI policy around their tools. If their IT teams get their way, they put everybody into Copilot, and that's not what we should be currently doing."*

Because here's the mic she drops on every client, and it hits hard every time: **"AI doesn't fix broken processes."**

If your data is dirty, AI will do analysis on dirty data. If your workflows aren't documented, AI will scale the confusion. If nobody knows who does what and when, adding AI is adding speed to chaos.

Kirsten Schmidtke, a sales leadership consultant, coach, and speaker, put it in a way that made me literally write it on a sticky note: *"If you're not clear about your processes, AI is going to scale the chaos."*

Buying a platform before you understand your workflows is how shelf-ware gets born. Audit first. Buy second.

The Tone That Makes or Breaks Your Audit

Before we get into the steps, we need to name the cultural trap that ruins many audits. If employees feel they are being questioned so they can be punished, they won't tell you the truth.

This is not a witch hunt. You're not here to scold anyone. You are here to build a current-state map so the organization can deal with risks without shutting everything down.

Jennifer Hufnagel reframed this beautifully. She told me that in her work, they do a software audit, a data audit, and a process audit. But they don't call it a people audit. Even though that's exactly what it is. Because *"your people know what's frustrating. They know what takes time. They're also nervous. But speaking to the people and finding out what they do day-to-day, and what problems they're trying to solve, that's really where we start."*

So. You want honesty? You need psychological safety. That doesn't mean 'anything goes'. It means your posture is curious and practical, not punitive.

A good audit produces honesty. Honesty requires trust. Trust comes from tone.

A Framework - The 4 Dimensions of an AI Audit

A good AI audit doesn't need to be a months-long compliance exercise. It also shouldn't be a purely technical inventory. What you're looking for is a coherent picture of AI activity across the organization. How it touches tools, workflows, people, and risk.

Dimension 1: Tools. What are we paying for? What's free? Where is AI already embedded in things we've had for years? Do they talk to each other?

Dimension 2: Workflows. How is work actually getting done, step by step? Where does AI show up? Where is the manual drudgery that's screaming for help?

Dimension 3: Adoption Patterns. Who are the power users? Who is dabbling? Who is avoiding it entirely, and why?

Dimension 4: Risks. Where is shadow AI? Where is sensitive information being handled unsafely? Where are governance gaps?

Each dimension tells a different truth. Together, they give you something most leaders don't have today: a grounded baseline. And once you have a baseline, you can stop arguing about hypotheticals and start making decisions based on evidence.

How to Run an AI Audit Without Boiling the Ocean

An audit works best when it is structured and time-boxed. Perfection is not the goal. Clarity is.

You can run a meaningful audit in weeks, not quarters, if you keep it focused and treat it as a leadership-level initiative, not a technical one.

Here's a simple sequence.

Step 1: Listen

Start with people. Always.

Run a short survey and a handful of interviews. Keep the questions clean and specific. Ask what tools people use for work. Ask what they use in their personal life too. Ask what use cases have been most helpful. Ask what worries them. Ask where they feel blocked. Ask what they wish leadership understood.

Then interview across the organization: department heads, AI champions, and (this is KEY) the skeptics. The people who may feel left behind. The people who don't trust the tools. The people who worry about job security or data risk. This is where you will hear truths your power users won't tell you.

Gazzy Amin, is the Founder of Sales Beyond Scripts, an entrepreneur and speaker whom I interviewed, and she shared a personal version of this that I loved. She described doing a 2025 audit using AI. She literally asked AI: *"Hey, I want to do a 2025 audit with you. Can you ask me a set of questions that will get you as much information as you need for us to do a deep dive on what worked, what didn't, and what I should focus on to scale?"*

And AI gave her a structured set of questions across finances, content, opportunities, speaking, partnerships. She told me: *"On my own, I wouldn't have come up with that."*

I love this example because it shows that the audit mindset isn't just for enterprises. Whether you're a team of 500 or a team of three, the question is the same: what's ACTUALLY happening, and what should we do next?

Listening is data collection. And it immediately signals to the organization that the audit is about reality, not performance.

Step 2: Map the Tools

Now you build the inventory.

List the official software and platforms you pay for that include AI capabilities. Then list the free and low-cost tools that have quietly entered the stack. Then identify overlaps: different departments paying for different tools that do similar things. Finally, document personal subscriptions being used for company work *(this will NOT be easy in large organizations so there will need to be some efforts created to break it down to departmental or sub-departmental levels)*.

This is the moment where leaders often get tempted to shut things down. We're resisting that reflex, remember? You are not trying to punish people for solving their own problems. You are trying to see what's true so you can decide what to formalize, what to replace, what to secure, and what to stop.

One of the most surprising outcomes of an audit is discovering that you've been using AI for YEARS without calling it AI. Resume filtering. Ticket triage. CRM suggestions. Auto-categorization in your support platform. Predictive features inside software you've been paying for since long before Gen AI became a thing.

This matters because it changes the narrative. You aren't suddenly 'starting AI'. You're surfacing what already exists and deciding how to govern it responsibly.

A note on the 'IT only' trap: Do NOT make your audit a purely IT exercise. IT matters, obvi. But this isn't only about infrastructure. It's about how people work, how information moves, and how cross-functional hand-offs happen under pressure. If the audit lives only in IT, you'll get a perfectly accurate map of licenses and zero understanding of how work is actually being done. This needs to start at a leadership level and move across departments.

Step 3: Document Workflows

Tools don't create ROI. Workflows do.

This step is where most of the value hides. Pick a few priority functions where AI is likely already in motion and where the business impact is high. Marketing, HR, and Sales are common starting points. Operations often follows.

Document the workflow step by step. Then mark where AI shows up. If it doesn't show up at all, mark that too.

As you do this, patterns emerge. You might discover: 'We use AI for first drafts, but still do all the research manually'. Or, 'We use AI to answer customer queries, but nobody reviews those transcripts'. Or, 'This process is 100% manual and we don't know where to start'.

Those patterns reveal your real opportunities. They also reveal your real risks.

Now, here's a thing that Kirsten Schmidtke and I talked about that surprised me: even in larger firms, clear sales processes or clear marketing SOPs don't necessarily exist. She said salespeople are great at execution, *"really good at executing. You want me to pick up the phone? Cold call? Go to an event? I will go do the thing every day."* But documenting how that works in a system? Not necessarily their skill set. Not their instinct.

She continued: *"Once you have it documented, you can start to identify what's working and what's not, and it gives you a really great place to start to see where AI can be integrated."*

Documentation before automation. Process before platform. Always.

Jennifer Hufnagel has a simple way she explains workflows to people who find the word intimidating: *"A workflow is really just a step-by-step and a checklist. You can explain what you do to a Generative AI Tool and ask it to create the procedure for you. Or you can go old school, take a stack of sticky notes, and go to a white board and map it out. This is the first step. This is the second step. Who does what, when?"*

If someone won the lottery tomorrow (and quit), could another person pick up their work from the documentation alone? If the answer is no, that's your starting point.

Step 4: Map Adoption Patterns

An AI audit is also a human behaviour audit. You need to know who is using AI confidently, who is dabbling, and who is avoiding it entirely. You need to know whether adoption is distributed across levels and departments, or concentrated in a few pockets.

This matters because it tells you what kind of training you need and where culture is working for you or against you. It surfaces your invisible champions and your quiet skeptics. Both of whom you need if you want sustainable adoption.

(Remember the archetype work from Chapter 4? This is where you start seeing your divers, pathfinders, operators, and bridge builders in the wild. The adoption map IS the archetype map, just with real names and real behaviour.)

Step 5: Assess Risk and Governance Gaps

Risk assessment comes next. Where is confidential or regulated data being touched by AI tools? Which teams are using public apps for sensitive work? What policies exist on paper? What's actually being practiced? Where are the gaps?

Helen Patterson, an HR leader I spoke with, told me a story that'll make readers do a double take. Because we'll recognize it. She'd been working with someone and had developed proprietary information. She then gave it to a colleague for feedback. And that person *uploaded it straight into a public AI tool*. Not maliciously. Not even carelessly, in their own mind. They just didn't know. And that's the thing. Most shadow AI isn't born from bad intentions. It's born from a gap between what people know and what people do. And the fact that any single workflow is touched by many hands, several of which might be external and not subject to the same rules as you.

Helen also pointed out something I see ALL the time: when organizations put really hard guardrails around AI, like 'you can only use Copilot, nothing else,' people just use their phones. *"Everyone has a phone"*, she said. And she's right. A blanket 'no' doesn't eliminate the behaviour. It just makes it invisible.

The goal of this step is not to shut everything down. It's to make safe behaviour easier than unsafe behaviour.

Step 6: Highlight Opportunities

The audit is not complete until it points forward.

Where are the quick wins? Where can AI save time and headspace? Where are emerging best practices that should be shared? Where are deeper opportunities to redesign workflows entirely?

The audit should surface not only risks but leverage. Because if all you hand leadership is a list of problems, you'll get fear. If you hand them problems AND opportunities, you'll get funding.

The Costs of Skipping the Audit

If you skip the audit and jump straight into tools or pilots, you'll typically pay for it in one (or more) of four ways. We covered this in detail in chapter 2. But here's a recap in the context of an AI audit.

1. Duplicate spend. Without visibility, different departments buy overlapping tools. Marketing pays for a content platform. Sales pays for another. HR pays for a third. Finance doesn't see the overlap because the spend is distributed. Leadership thinks the stack is lean. It isn't.

2. Governance risk. Employees pasting sensitive data into public LLMs. Documents going into unsanctioned tools. Personal devices, personal email, personal AI accounts being used for company work. It may seem fine until it isn't. And if you haven't mapped usage, you won't even know where to start cleaning it up.

3. Wasted efficiency gains. Some of the most valuable AI workflows live inside people's heads. A marketer who's cut planning time in half. A customer service rep who turns prep notes into action in minutes. A manager who does performance feedback faster and better. Without an audit, those efficiencies stay trapped. They don't become shared practice. They don't compound. The organization pays for learning that never scales.

4. No ROI story. If your CFO asks, 'What value are we getting from AI?' and you don't have an audit, you have no answer beyond anecdotes. An audit moves you from 'people feel faster' to 'cycle time dropped by 18% in these workflows'. It turns 'we think adoption is happening' into 'here's how many people have minimum viable AI literacy'. No audit means no ROI story. And without an ROI story, your AI flywheel doesn't get funded *(but more on that in chapter 7)*.

The Audit Output That Doesn't Die in a Folder

The goal is NOT a 90-slide deck that gathers dust. The goal instead is a working document leaders can use to make decisions and teams can use to build.

Part 1: Executive summary. Where are we now? Top risks and opportunities. Priorities for 3, 6, and 12 months.

Part 2: Tool and workflow map. What tools exist, where AI is embedded, overlaps, gaps, shadow usage, and the key workflows documented.

Part 3: Risk and governance assessment. Data, privacy, and regulatory concerns. Initial 'start, stop, continue' guidance.

Part 4: Opportunity backlog. Quick wins, experiments, and longer-term workflow redesign opportunities. Prioritized and ready for project management.

This document is your baseline. Your reality check. Your bridge from 'we think this' to 'we know this'.

Audit as the Middle of a Bigger Journey

Jennifer Hufnagel frames the whole AI journey in three stages: AI awareness, AI readiness, and AI adoption. The audit sits squarely in the readiness phase. *"AI readiness is looking at what is your existing software stack. What are all the pieces? Where is your data? How dirty is your data? It's mapping out workflows, processes, and tasks, determining your current state."*

Awareness is where people start playing and learning. Readiness is where you figure out what's true. Adoption is where you implement with confidence.

Too many organizations try to jump from awareness straight to adoption. They skip readiness entirely. And then they wonder why nothing sticks.

The audit IS the readiness step. It's not sexy. It's not glamorous. It's not going to make for a great LinkedIn post. *(Okay, maybe a small one. With a selfie!)*

But it's the foundation. And everything you build without it is built on guesswork.

Your Move: The 60-Minute Audit Starter

Block one hour this week. You are not trying to finish the audit. You are trying to START it. *(Pathfinders, I see you reaching for the two-day calendar block. One hour. Trust me.)*

Choose one function. Marketing, HR, Sales, or Operations.

Write down:

The tools they use that likely include AI (paid and free)

One workflow they repeat weekly

Where AI shows up in that workflow today

One risk you suspect exists

One opportunity you can test in the next 30 days

That's it. One page. One slice of the picture.

And if you want to try Gazzy Amin's approach, open up your AI tool of choice and say: 'I want to audit how my team is using AI right now. Can you ask me a set of questions to help me figure out what's actually happening?' You'll be a lot further than a blank page with what comes back from your AI.

Once you can see one slice clearly, it becomes easier to expand.

Remember, an audit isn't the end goal. It's the starting line.

Make the invisible stuff visible. Take those experiments trapped in people's heads and turn them into data points. Give your AI decisions a real foundation.

Because only THEN does it make sense to train your people, build or buy custom tools, and track ROI in a way that your CFO, your board, and your team will respect.

Stop guessing.

Start mapping.

The audit is your first real move.

Remember, this, and all the other mini exercises in this book are in one easy place for you to access. Scan the QR code below or visit: https://wearenorthlightai.com/swan-dive-backwards

CHAPTER 6

Training

Why one-off training fails, and what 'sticky literacy' actually looks like.

Let me guess.

Your organization runs AI 101 trainings from time to time. The session you went to was probably an hour long. Maybe a lunch and learn. Everyone clapped. Someone said 'game changer' like they'd just discovered electricity. There was laughter. Someone asked for the slide deck.

And then Monday arrived.

The inbox was full. The meetings multiplied. The work was impatient. And that bright, buzzy feeling from Friday dissolved into the familiar friction of 'I don't have time for this'.

That's the true test of training. Not the applause. Not the attendance. Not the screenshot of a prompt from the Zoom chat thread. The test is whether anything got easier on Monday morning.

(Spoiler: for most organizations, it didn't.)

The Monday Morning Test

Melissa Penton is a change manager at Sun Life in Ireland who also happens to be one of those rare folx who can translate between the tech world and the business world without making either side feel stupid. "*I am a purple person*", she says.

Melissa uses a question when she thinks about AI learning and change. It's not about adoption rates or tech stacks. It's not even about productivity.

It's simpler. And that's why it works.

What will make next Monday easier for you?
When training starts there, it becomes humane. It becomes concrete. It stops drifting into abstract demos and starts attaching itself to real pain. Real time. Real folx.

Melissa pushes back hard on the popular training goal of 'productivity'. Not because she's anti-results. Because she knows what happens when people hear 'productivity'. They hear: do more. Faster. Forever. They tune out. Or they comply and burn out. Her argument is: '*The real goal is to make room in your life for things that matter to you, and getting rid of all that busy work.*'

That might mean a better strategy. Better care. Better thinking. Or simply finishing work without carrying it into your evening.

If your training plan cannot answer the Monday Morning question in plain language, you're not building capability.

Why One-Off Training Fails

One-off AI training fails for the same reason one workout fails.

You can have a great session. You can feel inspired. You can buy new shoes. Then life resumes. Habits pull you back. The calendar crowds out intention. The body returns to what it knows.

AI learning behaves the same way. ESPECIALLY for busy leaders and founder-led teams who don't have the luxury of 'play time' that isn't connected to outcomes.

One-off sessions typically create two predictable groups.

Group A leaves overconfident. They think AI is a vending machine: put a prompt in, receive a perfect answer out. When the output is generic, wrong, or risky, they still ship it. Quality drops. Trust drops. Adoption stalls.

Group B leaves intimidated. They decide, quietly, 'AI isn't for me'. They never get enough reps to build confidence, so avoidance becomes their strategy. And avoidance compounds FAST.

Neither group creates sustainability. And if you've read Chapter 3, you'll recognize this as the literacy divide in action. The gap between Group A and Group B widens every single week. Because nobody built the system to hold the learning.

Melissa Penton nailed this when she told me: *'AI is just being thrown at people and people are not ready for it. They don't know how to change. They don't know what to do.'* It's noisy. It's corporate-heavy. And people can't figure out how it fits into their actual lives.

The Login Trap

Here's the most common 'we're doing something' move that leaders make while believing they're being responsible.

Buy licenses. Distribute access. Schedule a workshop. Assume enablement is complete.

Except access is not enablement.

Shona Boyd, who we met in the Chapter 3 literacy gap conversation, put it as bluntly as possible: *'Don't just hand out logins to tools with no written policy and no clarity on what is acceptable to put into those tools.'* That isn't training. That's a breach waiting to happen.

And Shona goes further. She's seen it from the inside. The unapproved note-takers joining meetings. The personal ChatGPT accounts being used to analyze company data. *'There's a lot more people doing it than you think,'* she told me. *'If you say we will not use AI, everyone's going to probably use it behind your back.'*

We covered the shadow AI problem in Chapter 2 and the governance gaps in Chapter 5. This would be a good time to review those chapters if it's been a while since you read them.

The training implication is this: when the safe path isn't clear, people improvise. When they improvise without guidance, they either create risk or they avoid the tool entirely. If you want safe behaviour at scale, you have to make the safe path the easiest path. That begins with guardrails that feel like guidance, not policing.

You're Teaching a Language, Not a Feature Set

This is the shift that separates training that sticks from training that evaporates.

Traditional software training teaches buttons and steps. Where to click. What sequence to follow. Learn it once, repeat it forever. The interface stays mostly stable.

AI training is different because you aren't learning features. You're learning a language. You're learning how to think clearly, describe what you want, add context, notice what's missing, verify what matters, and refine instead of accepting the first output like it's a verdict.

Suzanne Huber, a go-to-market consultant and one of my regular co-working partners, has this phrase I adore. She was at dinner with her sister and friends, and some people at the table were saying they were freaked out by AI. And her sister said: '*Why don't you want to use your robot arms?*'

Robot arms. I love that so much.

Because that's exactly what AI is. An extension of your expertise. But here's the thing Suzanne was clear about: '*You still need to use critical thinking. You still need to know the difference between good and bad. You don't take the first draft.*'

And she's a writer who's been doing this for over 15 years. She told me she gave a client two pieces of writing. One mostly written by her. One mostly by AI, after several iterations and push-backs. '*They picked the AI one over my own writing.*' But that only worked because she knew how to shape it. Because the iteration WAS the expertise.

Jennifer Hufnagel, who we leaned on heavily in Chapter 5, described AI as *"a sparring partner, a collaborator, sometimes even a temporary Co-CEO."*

"If you treat it like a search engine, you'll be disappointed. If you treat it like a collaborator you can steer and correct, you'll improve quickly. The real skill is learning how to work the draft and knowing what can be delegated to AI and where human oversight still matters.

This is also where we need to talk about the shift from prompt engineering to something more durable. Melissa Penton calls it context engineering. Her point: *"It shouldn't be about how often people are using the tool. It should be around, are they asking better questions overall? Are they more thoughtful?"* The deeper skill is the human ability to provide the right background, ask sharper questions, and steer a conversation toward something useful.

The machine can't rescue unclear thinking. It can only amplify it.

The Readiness Gate (Check Before you Train)

Before you build training, pass through a simple gate. It will save you time, money, and disappointment.

If you did the audit work from Chapter 5, you already have most of this. If you skipped it (no judgement), you'll need to answer these questions before training will stick:

Guardrails exist in writing. People can find them without asking three different people.

At least one real workflow is visible. Not perfect. Just mapped end-to-end. (Chapter 5, Step 3.)

Leaders participate. Not just sponsor. They practise. They model learning. (More on this in a second.)

Time is protected. Learning is part of work, not extra time.

A first win is defined. Monday gets easier in a specific way.

If you can't meet these conditions yet, that's ok. It tells you what to fix before you ask people to practise. Because training is a multiplier. It multiplies whatever reality already exists. If the reality is unclear policy, invisible workflows, and no protected time, training multiplies confusion.

Framework: The 4 Layers of Sticky Literacy

If you want AI literacy to survive past Tuesday, you need a system. Here are the four layers I use because they align with how humans actually learn. (Not how we WISH they learned. How they actually do.)

Layer 1: Safety and Policy

Layer 2: Shared Vocabulary

Layer 3: Workflow Practice

Layer 4: Rituals

Notice what's missing from this list: hype and news cycles. Also missing: perfection.

Not everyone needs to become an AI engineer. Good training is a floor, not a ceiling. You're building a baseline where everyone can safely participate, speak the language, and contribute use cases.

Let's make each one real.

Layer 1: Safety and Policy

Before you teach prompts, teach boundaries. People cannot practise safely if they don't know what 'safe' means. In many organizations, the policy either doesn't exist yet, exists in legal language nobody reads, or exists as a vague caution that people interpret as fear.

Your training needs to translate policy into daily behaviour. Not a 40-page document. Three lines that every person on your team can recite from memory:

> **Never allowed:** What data never goes into AI tools? (Names, account numbers, health records, whatever applies to your context.)
>
> **Allowed with caution:** What requires review, anonymization, or a second set of eyes?
>
> **Safe by default:** What can your team use freely and openly?

When people know the boundaries, they practise proudly. They share learning. They ask better questions. When boundaries are vague, people practise privately and hope for the best.

Layer 2: Shared Vocabulary

A shared vocabulary prevents chaos. If half your team says 'agent' and means 'automation', and the other half says 'agent' and means 'magic little robot that does everything', you will have endless misalignment. If people don't know the difference between a draft and a decision, they will treat output as truth. If people don't understand hallucinations, they won't know when to verify.

Shona Boyd put it simply: *'Having some foundational understanding of the terms will make you feel a little more included in the conversation. So you're not like, oh, I don't know what that person is talking about, and feel intimidated.'*

Vocabulary is not jargon for its own sake, it's alignment. And it reduces shame. AI can make smart people feel slow. Naming that reality out loud changes everything. It makes learning socially safe, which is the only kind of learning that scales inside an organization.

And while we're on vocabulary: can we please stop calling training courses things like 'AI Agents for the Enterprise'? Melissa Penton was passionate about this: *'I'm very allergic to that kind of conversation. These are not words in our vocabulary at the moment.'* If you name your training in language that makes people want to call in sick, you've already lost.

Layer 3: Workflow Practice

This is the layer most organizations skip. And it's the one that creates traction. The latest AI toy demos are seductive. Generating a flashy output in 30 seconds looks impressive. It also does nothing for the work your team actually has to do on Monday.

Training becomes sticky when it attaches to real repetition: the tasks your team does weekly, the friction that keeps resurfacing, the manual drudgery that drains the best thinking out of your best people.

Which is why generic prompt packs are such a trap. They don't know your context. They don't know your voice. They don't know your policies. They don't know what 'good' looks like in your organization. In the case of many small teams of 1-5, I'll hear about how they bought a prompt pack from an Instagram ad because it promised so much. Or maybe one of the big AI names in your LinkedIn feed regularly posts prompts they think you should try and you have a folder full of screenshots waiting. You tried one. And the output came out nothing like theirs.

It's like borrowing someone else's meal plan and expecting it to fit your body. Inspiring? Maybe. Precise? Not a chance.

Here's what workflow practice actually looks like. Jennifer Hufnagel told me that the core of her programs is helping people have their individual 'AI aha moment.' Not in theory. In their role. *'We spend a lot of time figuring out how you could use these tools for YOUR role',* she said.

Layer 4: Rituals

If you don't create cadence, your old habits will win. This is the layer that separates organizations who train from organizations who transform. Because AI training is change management. You're changing behaviour. And behaviour change only sticks when there's a container to hold it.

Back to that gym analogy. You can have one INCREDIBLE session. Endorphins flying. New playlist. Feel like a superhero. Then day two comes and you're sore and the alarm goes off and it's snowing outside and you're like, I'm worth it, I'm going to sleep in.

(Ask me how I know.)

The fix is a system: a time, a rhythm, an accountability loop, and a community where the behaviour is normal.

Melissa Penton says: *'Experiential learning is going to be the thing. People need to learn by experience. This is not a technology that you can sit and talk about theoretically in a room. You really need people to have the tactile experience of using it and trying it and seeing how it works for them.'*

So. Weekly loops. Not monthly. Not quarterly. Weekly.

Build the Editor Mindset

If there's one skill your training needs to build above all else, it's the ability to look at AI output and say: what's wrong? What's missing? What's risky? What's too generic? What needs verification?

And then re-prompt. Refine. Steer.

Suzanne Huber spotlights this: *'The first output that comes out, there's no way I'm letting anyone see it. There's no way it's going beyond my eyes.'* And she's been writing professionally for 15 years. If she's not trusting the first draft, nobody should be.

She also made the point about what happens when the editor mindset is MISSING: *'That's where the threat for the future is. If people just believe that everything is factually true and blindly go in and use outputs from AI, you're going to get different recommendations from different platforms.'* You can't just say 'ChatGPT told me to do this' and call it a strategy.

The goal is to shape content, not meaninglessly generate it in buckets. And shaping requires reps. Which brings us to the how.

Building Training That Actually Changes Monday

If I were sitting across from you as a consultant right now *(probably with a coffee that's gone cold because I forgot about it again)*, here's the roadmap I'd walk you through. It's practical. It's designed to create reps. And it avoids the two outcomes you don't want: overconfidence and intimidation.

Step 1: Define the Outcome

Training without an outcome is a motivational speech.

Write this sentence down: 'In 60 days, AI will help our team ____.'

Then write: 'We will know it worked when ____.'

Choose one: reduce cycle time, improve quality, reduce risk, improve customer response, improve decision making.

If you can't fill those in, don't start training yet.

Start with strategy. *(And maybe revisit the audit from Chapter 5.)*

Step 2: Put Guardrails Before Prompts

Before you teach people how to talk to the machine, tell them what they can safely bring into the room. The three-line framework from Layer 1: never allowed, allowed with caution, safe by default. Make it visible. Make it repeatable. Laminate it and stick it on the wall if you have to.

Step 3: Pick a Practice Lane

Training becomes sticky when it attaches to repetition. Have your team list three high-repetition workflows. The work you do every week. The work that is frequent, annoying, and low-risk. Then circle one. That becomes your first training target.

(Proposals. Client summaries. Internal comms. Research briefs. Onboarding docs. Meeting notes. Performance feedback. Whatever your team repeats. Circle the one that hurts the most.)

Melissa Penton's Monday Morning question guides this: '*What are your tension points at work? What would make it easier? Let's have those conversations so that you can start asking better questions.*'

The point is to build confidence in work that actually matters. Not on toy demos that look cool and accomplish nothing.

Step 4: Run the 'Real Work' Loop

This is the heart of training. Where literacy becomes muscle.

The loop:

Bring one real task. Not hypothetical.

Prompt once. Accept the ugly first draft. (It's GOING to be ugly. And when I say draft I don't mean only writing. It could be a plan or action of any sort.)

Critique like an editor: what's wrong, missing, risky, too generic?

Re-prompt to improve.

Share the before and after with your team.

Do this weekly for eight weeks and your organization will change. However big or small your organization is. Because the habit becomes normal. Because the editor mindset develops through reps, not lectures. Because people start to see their own thinking get sharper.

Step 5: Build a Community of Practice

This is how you prevent the backslide. Jennifer Hufnagel says, "*There's something beautiful about bringing people together from different industries, even at your company, learning from each other to figure out and solve the challenges. Your people know. We just need to ask them and enable them.*"

You need champions. But not in the heroic sense. Not one genius who carries the team. That model burns people out and creates dependency. You want curious catalysts. Two per team is a better number than one. One is too lonely. Two can sustain each other and share the load.

These catalysts don't need to be the most technical people in the room. Melissa Penton would tell you the best ones are often the 'purple people'. The translators. The ones who live between the tech world and the business world. Their job is to keep practice visible. And PROTECT them. If your training strategy depends on invisible labour from people who volunteered because they're enthusiastic, it will eventually collapse. Give them time. Give them credit. Give them partners.

The Personal Aha (Why Home Use Matters)

As an intuitive leader, here's something to regularly call to mind. People often need a PERSONAL 'aha' before they can confidently use AI at work. Shona Boyd shared an example that stayed with me. She's part of the sandwich generation and helps take care of her grandmother. She knew nothing about Medicare at the time. So she downloaded the dense PDF from the government website, uploaded it to an AI, and started asking questions. *'Did you know you can do that?'* she said. *'It will reference that material.'* Then she did the same thing with her credit card rewards. Took a picture of the fine print packet, uploaded it, and asked: *'Am I really getting something back, or should I downgrade my card?'*

These are LIFE tasks. And they matter for training because they build confidence in a lower-stakes environment. Once someone trusts themselves with their Medicare questions, they bring that confidence into their work proposals. The skill transfers. The fear reduces. The questions improve.

Your Move: The Monday Morning Training Brief

Do this with one team. Fifteen minutes. Paper only. *(Yes, paper. The irony is intentional.)*

Monday win: 'Next Monday would be easier if we could _____.'

Proof: 'We'll know it worked when _____.'

Guardrails: Never allowed/Allowed with caution/Safe by default. Three lines.

Practice lane: One workflow that is frequent, annoying, and low-risk.

Cadence: One weekly 30-minute session for eight weeks. On the calendar. *(If it isn't scheduled, it doesn't exist.)*

Catalysts: Two people per team. Curious, not expert. Purple, not perfect.

If you can't fill this in, don't schedule training yet. Tighten readiness first. Go back to the audit. Go back to the Readiness Gate. Do the ground work. THEN build the training.

But if you CAN fill it in? Start this week. Not next quarter. This week.

This, and all the other mini exercises in this book are in one easy place for you to access. Scan the QR code below or visit: https://wearenorthlightai.com/swan-dive-backwards

CHAPTER 7

The AI Flywheel

How to turn experiments into compounding momentum.

Let me tell you the language that makes me nervous. Pilot. Initiative. Six-week sprint. Phase one. Test project. AI Budget line.

All perfectly reasonable words. All describing things that are built to END.

And that's the problem. Because AI is not a project. It's not a thing you launch, applaud, and file away. It's not an ERP implementation from 2008 where you go live, send the company-wide email with the confetti emoji, and then move on with your life.

AI is a compounding system. Or at least, it should be. And if you treat it like a project, you'll get exactly what projects deliver: a burst of enthusiasm, a stall, a dose of scepticism, and then the quiet, depressing return to 'the old way'.

We've been building toward this chapter. Chapter 5 gave you the audit. Chapter 6 gave you the training. Chapter 4 showed you how to lead the different people who'll be doing this work. Now we need the system that connects all of it.

Not a strategy deck. Not a one-time initiative.

A flywheel.

Projects End. Flywheels Compound.

A project has a beginning, a middle, and a finish line. It comes with a launch plan and a comforting sense of closure. Everyone loves the Gantt chart. Everyone loves the 'complete' checkbox. Leaders chase 'the big moment'. Teams wait for permission. Success is defined by completion rather than capability building.

And then it's done. And everyone moves on. Maybe nothing changes on Monday.

A flywheel is different.

A flywheel is a giant metal wheel. Heavy. Stubborn. It takes real effort to get the first turn going. You push and push and it barely moves. It feels pointless. You wonder if it's broken. *(It isn't. It's physics.)*

But once it starts spinning, each turn adds momentum. The energy you put in accumulates. The wheel gets easier to turn, not harder. And eventually, it becomes really, really hard to stop.

THAT is what sustainable AI adoption needs to feel like. An accumulation of consistent effort, in the same direction.

This isn't a new idea. Jim Collins brought flywheels into business language decades ago in his book ***'Good to Great'***. Apply that thinking to AI adoption. Stop treating AI as a moonshot announcement. Stop treating it as a vendor contract. Start treating it as momentum.

No one is making a documentary about your small wins. I know that. I know it's less exciting than the big launch. But when you stack small wins consistently in the same direction? That's when it compounds. That's when you build an advantage that competitors can't copy by buying a license.

The Moonshot Trap

Let's name this one because I see it EVERYWHERE. Leaders love a big moment. A vendor contract with a press release attached. A dramatic pilot with executive sponsorship and a slide deck that makes it look like the future has arrived. An all-hands meeting where someone says 'we're doing AI now' with the energy of a TED talk and the specificity of a horoscope.

Here's what happens with the moonshot: you get a spike of activity. Excitement. Maybe some early wins. Then the spike fades. The organization interprets the fade as failure. Leadership gets cautious. Budget gets tighter. And the narrative becomes 'we tried AI, and it didn't really stick'.

But it DIDN'T fail. What failed was the FORMAT. The initiative was built like a project. It had a start and an end. And when the end came, nobody had built the system to keep it spinning.

The alternative is less glamorous. WAY less glamorous. It's one use case that works. One workflow that reduces drudgery. One dashboard that makes progress visible. One team that can point to a number and say: this changed. The flywheel needs consistent turns.

Framework: The 4 Pillars of the AI Flywheel

At a high level, the flywheel has four pillars in motion. On paper, they look linear. In reality, they behave like a loop. Your results feed the next audit. Your audit shapes training. Training unlocks better workflows. Better workflows produce measurable ROI. That ROI funds the next turn.

Pillar 1: Audit. Where are we really?

Pillar 2: Training. Raise the floor of literacy.

Pillar 3: Personalized Tools. Workflows over generic chatbots.

Pillar 4: ROI. The story that keeps the wheel funded.

And around all four, like a ring holding the whole thing together: **culture**.

Let's make each pillar practical. Not theory. Not hype. A way of working you can return to every quarter, even as the tools change underneath you. *(And they will. Oh, they will.)*

Pillar 1: Audit (The Reality Check)

We went deep on this in Chapter 5. *(You're welcome.)* The flywheel context adds something important. Your audit is not a one-time event. It's a recurring discipline.

The first audit tells you where you are. The second audit, maybe six months later, tells you what changed. The third tells you what's compounding and what stalled. Each audit adjusts your understanding as the environment shifts. Because the environment WILL shift. New tools will arrive. Old tools will add features nobody asked for. Someone on your team will have quietly built something brilliant. Someone else will have quietly created a risk. The audit catches all of it.

Think of it as a regular reality check. Not a punishment. Not a compliance exercise. A moment to look up from the work and say: where are we actually? Not where we hoped we'd be. Not where the vendor dashboard says we are. Where we ACTUALLY are.

That grounded starting point is what makes every other pillar honest.

Quick reminder of what the audit maps *(the full breakdown is in Chapter 5 if you need it)*: tools already in play, workflows people have invented, risks and data-handling realities, and whatever guardrails exist, even informally.

For the full audit template and all the other mini exercises in this book, scan the QR code below or visit: https://wearenorthlightai.com/swan-dive-backwards

If your last audit was more than six months ago, it's time for another one.

Pillar 2: Training (Building the Floor)

We went deep on this one too, in Chapter 6. So again, I'll be brief and focus on what the flywheel adds. Training in the flywheel is not a one-time activity. It's a continuously improving system that responds to what the audit reveals.

The first round of training builds the floor. Minimum viable literacy. Safety and policy. Shared vocabulary. Workflow practice. Rituals. *(Chapter 6 has the whole system.)*

But here's the flywheel piece: each audit cycle should reshape the NEXT round of training. Maybe the first round taught people how to use AI for drafting. The second round, six months later, teaches them how to build workflows. The third round starts to explore more advanced use cases. Each round builds on the last.

This is also how you avoid the stale training trap. You know the one. 'We already did AI training in 2024'. Great. What was true in 2024 is not entirely true in 2026 or 2028. The tools changed. The capabilities changed. Your people changed. The training has to keep pace. EXPONENTIALLY in the case of AI.

Not in a panicky, start-from-scratch kind of way. In a flywheel kind of way. Each turn refines what came before.

The other thing training feeds into the flywheel is PEOPLE. When you train well, you surface your divers, your pathfinders, your operators, your bridge builders. *(Remember them from Chapter 4?)* You find out who's ready to prototype, who's ready to document, who's ready to scale. The training creates the talent map for Pillar 3.

Pillar 3: Personalized Tools (Workflow First, Tool Second)

This is where the flywheel starts to feel REAL. When people stop using AI only as a generic chat window and start building workflows, your wins become repeatable. Repeatable wins are shareable. Shareable wins are scalable. This is the moment adoption stops being conceptual and becomes operational.

There's lots of talk about agents. In early 2026, 'agents' are imagined as these magical little workers that run entire processes end-to-end, maybe bringing you a coffee while they're at it. And sure, we may get there in some contexts. But for most organizations, a more grounded way to think about it is this: a series of smaller processes strung together, with the manual drudgery removed.

Call prep. Account research. Proposal drafts. Onboarding steps. Campaign planning. Customer support summaries. Meeting follow-ups. Content repurposing.

These are workflows. That's all an 'agent' really is at this stage: a workflow that can run with less human grunt work.

Start asking: 'what does this 37-step process look like if we remove the parts that make people want to scream?'

THAT question is where the leverage lives.

In many organizations, the tool decision has already been made for you. If you live in a Microsoft universe, you likely have Copilot. Google universe? Gemini. And very few people who are in a 9-5 role are able to use any kind of open source tool at work. These defaults are embedded in what you already pay for and the need for data security. The decision happened whether you were thinking about it or not.

The strategic work, then, is not debating the abstract 'best tool' in a meeting room for six months. *(Please don't do this. I'm begging you.)* The strategic work is personalizing the defaults into workflows that actually fit YOUR business model.

When that happens, the flywheel accelerates.

The sequence that matters:

Map the workflow first. Identify the manual drudgery. THEN decide what to buy, build, or bolt on. When leaders reverse this order (picking tools first and hoping workflows magically appear), adoption becomes fragile and expensive.

A tool without a workflow is a shiny object. A workflow without the right tool can still be valuable, because at minimum you've clarified the work. Clarity is never wasted.

Pillar 4: ROI (The Story That Keeps the Wheel Funded)

ROI is where many AI initiatives go to die. Not because they aren't delivering value. Because the organization can't TELL THE STORY of that value convincingly.

Leaders look for a dramatic payoff. A million-dollar savings. A head-count reduction. A single 'wow' moment they can put in a board presentation. And when AI doesn't deliver that clean, cinematic narrative, they assume it isn't working.

In practice, ROI tends to show up as a stack of smaller wins: time saved, errors reduced, faster time to market, smoother hand-offs, fewer preventable mistakes, less rework, better decisions. Individually, none of these makes the front page. Collectively, they change the math of your business.

Let me give you a tiny example from my own world. Proofreading. Humans make mistakes. Typos used to be common, and catching them was real labour. Now, between built-in tools and language models, error detection has become widely available. In a handful of years, we've reduced something that used to consume meaningful time and reputation risk. That is ROI. It's not flashy. It IS compounding.

Faster time to market is another one. There has NEVER been a time when you could take an idea to market with strong supporting materials in a fraction of the time it used to take. Should everyone race? No. But the capability shift is real, and if your competitors are on this flywheel and you aren't, the gap is widening every month.

Risk reduction is also ROI, and it's the one people forget. If you build governance and policy adoption in a way that protects data and intellectual property while enabling innovation, that's value. If you reduce the likelihood of an incident, that's value. If you increase responsible behaviour at scale, that's value. It just doesn't have a dollar sign attached to it, which is why nobody puts it on the hero slide.

Metrics That Actually Matter

You need a handful of metrics that are meaningful enough to keep leadership engaged and honest enough to tell you when something isn't working.

Hours saved per week (per role or team). The simplest and most powerful. If a workflow used to take an hour and now takes ten minutes, do the math across a team. Across a month. Across a year. It compounds fast.

Error reduction rates. Rework. Typos. Compliance misses. Anything that used to go wrong because a human was tired, rushed, or overwhelmed.

Faster time to market. Cycle time reductions. How long does it take to go from brief to deliverable? From idea to proposal? From draft to approval? If those numbers are shrinking, you're winning.

Risk reduction. Policy adoption. Fewer incidents. Safer data handling. Less shadow AI. (Yes, 'less shadow AI' is a metric. If your audit shows it's declining, your governance is working.)

% of staff with minimum viable AI literacy. This one matters more than people realize. It tells you whether you're building a floor or leaving people behind. If the number is low, the flywheel won't spin because half the organization isn't participating.

Number of AI-augmented workflows in active use. Not 'how many tools do we have'. How many WORKFLOWS are actually running? This is the adoption number that matters.

Treat your point of measurement less like surveillance and more like momentum. People keep funding what they can understand. They keep supporting what they can see.

And if your CFO or board asks 'what value are we getting from AI?' *(they will)*, your answer is not an anecdote. It's a dashboard. We talked about the cost of skipping the audit in Chapter 5. No audit equals no baseline. No baseline equals no ROI story. No ROI story equals no funding. This is the pillar that keeps the flywheel turning when the initial excitement fades.

The ROI of 'Good Enough'

Can we talk about perfectionism for a second? Because I see it everywhere in AI conversations and it is KILLING momentum.

'We need the perfect agent.'

'We need the perfect policy before we start training.'

'We need the perfect workflow before we show leadership.'

No, you don't.

You need a workflow that takes a manual task from one hour down to ten minutes. You need a policy that covers 80% of the use cases. You need an agent that handles the repetitive parts of one workflow well enough that humans can focus on the parts that require judgement.

'Good enough' done consistently is more valuable than 'perfect' that never ships.

(I feel strongly about this. Can you tell?)

The flywheel is forgiving. You don't need perfection in the first turn. You need movement. The second turn refines. The third turn optimizes. The tenth turn is where people look at your operation and say, 'how did they get so far ahead?' And the answer is: they started. Imperfectly. Early. And they didn't stop.

Culture: The Ring Around the Flywheel

Here's where I need to get a little fierce. You can have all four pillars humming. Audit done. Training rolling. Workflows live. ROI visible. And the flywheel can STILL stall.

Because the flywheel is your engine. Culture is your operating system. You can have a Ferrari engine, but if the OS is glitchy (fear, silence, lack of trust, blame, exhaustion), the engine won't spin.

We've touched on culture throughout this book. The shame gap from Chapter 3. The psychological safety needed for audits in Chapter 5. The tone that makes training feel safe instead of threatening in Chapter 6. Culture is the thing that holds it all together.

These three things that kill the flywheel culturally.

1. Governance that feels like policing. If your rules feel punitive, people will hide their experiments. Shadow AI will increase. The data you need for the audit will go underground. We covered this and here's a reminder. Governance needs to feel like guidance, not punishment. Safe behaviour has to be the EASIEST path, not the heroic one.

2. Power users burning out as unpaid help desks. This one happens so quietly. A few enthusiastic people get great at AI. Word spreads. Suddenly everyone's in their DMs asking for help. Their own work suffers. Their enthusiasm curdles. They stop sharing because sharing turned into a second job nobody's paying them for. The flywheel cannot be fuelled by burnout. If you noticed this pattern in Chapter 4 with the divers, it's the same dynamic. Protect your champions. Build mentorship. Reward documentation. Make learning a collective behaviour, not a private tax paid by your most capable people.

3. Accidental hustle culture. A flywheel can quietly create pressure if you don't design for humanity. Leaders get excited about wins. The organization starts optimizing for speed. Nobody notices that 'efficiency gains' is slowly becoming code for 'do more with the same people at the same pay, faster'. That is not the promise. The promise *(remember Melissa Penton's framing from Chapter 6?)* is clearing busy work so people have room for what matters. If the flywheel just means more output, same humans, no breathing room, you don't have a flywheel. You have a hamster wheel.

(And yes, I did just call out an entire category of organizational behaviour as a hamster wheel. I stand by it.)

The Compounding Advantage

Loath as I am to give you a tired big tech example, here we are. Think Amazon for a hot second. They've been deploying AI for a WHILE. Not 'launch' AI once and move on. They built a recommendation flywheel. Customers clicked. Data improved. Recommendations got better. Sales increased. Then the loop repeated. The details of that technology have evolved. The structure of the advantage has not.

That's the point. You are not trying to 'adopt AI'. You are trying to build a compounding loop inside your organization where each turn makes the next one easier, smarter, and more effective.

You don't need to be Amazon. *(Thank god, because no.)* You just need to be consistent.

The organizations that will be in the strongest position in 2027 and beyond will be the ones that built the tightest loops between auditing, training, building, and measuring. The ones where every win fed the next experiment. Where every experiment fed the next capability. Where every capability fed the next business case.

That's the flywheel. It calls stubbornness in the right direction.

How to Start the Wheel

You don't build flywheels in a day. You start with a centimetre of movement. Sit down with a few leaders and ask these questions. *(Real talk. Not a strategy deck. A conversation.)*

Is AI a separate plan, or a thread through everything? If it's siloed in one department or one 'AI initiative', it will behave like a project. If it's woven into how every function thinks about work, it behaves like a flywheel. However it does need points of ownership.

Are we doing one-off sessions, or building real literacy? You already know the answer from Chapter 6. But it's worth asking out loud, because sometimes organizations say 'we're building literacy' when what they mean is 'we did a lunch-and-learn in March last year'.

Are we tracking impact, or just activity? 'Number of AI licenses purchased' is activity. 'Hours saved per week in the marketing team' is impact. What you did with those hours is LEGACY. Know the difference.

Where is AI already in motion, quietly, today? Your Chapter 5 audit answers this. But if you haven't done the audit yet, just ask. You'll be surprised.

What would one workflow look like with the manual drudgery removed? Pick the most annoying, repetitive, time-sucking workflow your team has. Now imagine it without the parts that make people groan. That's your first turn.

How will we measure the difference? Even a rough metric is better than none. 'This used to take 3 hours, now it takes 45 minutes' is a real number. Use it.

Then choose one small turn and commit to it. One audit. One workflow. One dashboard. Repeat.

The flywheel needs consistency, not perfection.

Your Move: Your First Centimetre

Pick one team. Pick one workflow. Give yourself 30 days.

Week 1: Quick audit. Where is AI already showing up in this workflow, officially or unofficially? What tools are in play? What's manual that shouldn't be? (If you did the Chapter 5 exercise, you have a head start.)

Week 2: Training pulse. What do people on this team need to use AI safely and effectively in this workflow? Guardrails. Vocabulary. One practice session. (Chapter 6's framework applies.)

Week 3: Build one workflow. Design a personalized workflow that reduces the manual drudgery in this one area. Not a whole system. One workflow. Keep it tight.

Week 4: Measure and share. Track one metric that matters. Hours saved. Errors reduced. Cycle time shortened. Then report it back to leadership. Make it visible.

Do NOT over-scope this. The point is momentum, not theatre. You're not trying to transform the entire organization in 30 days. You're trying to get one centimetre of movement on the flywheel.

Because once it moves, it's easier to push again.

This, and all the other mini exercises in this book are in one easy place for you to access. Scan the QR code below or visit: https://wearenorthlightai.com/swan-dive-backwards

The Wheel Doesn't Need a Documentary

No one is making a documentary about your small wins. I know. There won't be a conference keynote about how your sales team saved four hours a week on proposal prep. Nobody's putting 'we reduced our customer response cycle time by 22%' on a billboard.

But stack those wins in the same direction, month after month, quarter after quarter, and something happens that's much more powerful than a keynote.

The wheel starts to spin.

And once it spins, it becomes very, very hard for competitors to catch up. Because they can't buy your flywheel in LinkedIn ads. They can't license your culture. They can't hire your momentum. They have to build their own. From scratch. While yours is already turning.

Start the wheel.

One centimetre.

This month.

CHAPTER 8

Culture as the OS

AI is the app. Culture is the operating system.

Here's a sentence I need you to sit with for a second. **If you don't design values, norms, and expectations around AI, your culture will design itself.**

And self-designed culture is never tidy. It's shaped by rumours, hallway advice, private experiments, and the unspoken social rules of what gets you in trouble. That's nowhere close to governance.

Instead what's happening is a gentle drift that nobody really feels and after some time the organization ends up with three different versions of reality running at the same time, none of which leadership can see.

We've built the engine in the last few chapters. The audit *(Chapter 5)* told you where you are. The training *(Chapter 6)* raised the floor. The flywheel *(Chapter 7)* connected everything into a compounding system.

Now we need the operating system those pieces run on.

Because, you can have a Ferrari engine. But if the OS is glitchy (fear, silence, blame, exhaustion), the engine won't spin, remember?

AI is the app. Culture is the operating system.

And you can't download a culture update from a vendor.

AI Adoption Is a Human System

AI is used by people. People with fears and pride and habits. People who respond to incentives. People who conceal uncertainty when it feels unsafe. People who share learning when it feels valued.

While this is starting to read like a motivational poster, it's really organizational physics.

When leaders ask, *'Why isn't adoption sticking?',* the answer is almost never technical. It's cultural.

If people don't feel safe asking questions, confusion turns into silence. If people don't know what's allowed, experimentation turns into risk. If people don't see how AI connects to outcomes that matter, it becomes optional. And if people don't trust the output, they quietly redo the work by hand and tell themselves AI is *'fine, but not for us'*.

Helen Patterson has spent 25 years in the people business. You've met her earlier in this book. She's an HR leader who specializes in building 'heart-centred, high-performing cultures' for scaling businesses. She's also the author of *Create a Mentor Culture,* which tells you where her heart is. She's been through Y2K, the dot-com era, every wave of HR technology. And now AI.

Her read on this moment? It's evolution, not revolution. *'We have been talking about technology as an enabler for years',* she told me. *'This is just another evolution of that. How do we use artificial intelligence to alleviate all that day-to-day grunt work, so that we can actually help people grow?'*

That framing matters. Technology as enabler, not replacement. *'Let's not forget that the ideas come first from a human',* Helen said. *'Your creativity is not going to change.'* What changes is how much space you have for it.

But here's what Helen also knows after decades of watching organizations navigate change: space doesn't materialize by accident. You have to build the culture that makes it safe to use new tools, safe to ask questions, safe to be new at something. And if you don't build it? People will use the tools anyway. Just not safely. And not visibly.

Why the Experiment Era Makes Culture Visible

Earlier in this book *(Chapter 2, for the folx keeping score)*, we named the Experiment Era: the period where AI use is energetic, uneven, and often invisible to leadership. Not a calendar phase. A behaviour phase. Early adopters move through it quickly. Later adopters may live there for years.

The Experiment Era is a necessary stage. It's where curiosity creates real learning. It's also where the fault lines in your culture become IMPOSSIBLE to ignore.

When culture is absent, two things happen. Both are predictable. Both are preventable.

You get shadow AI. People use tools the organization doesn't know about. They do it because the work still needs to get done and curiosity finds oxygen. (*We covered this in Chapter 2.*)

You get the AI literacy divide. Some people become power users. Others don't know where to begin, or feel too embarrassed to ask. The gap widens. Adoption stalls, not because AI 'doesn't work,' but because your organization now has two realities living side by side. (*Chapter 3 laid this out in detail. This will continue to be an issue in organizations whether you read this book when it's published or 5 years after. I'd bet money on it. Why? Because think how long it took for online banking to fully take. After 20 years banks had to quite literally refuse to look at paper products or pity-look at them for elder, long-termers. Because their mamas raised them right and it was too much trouble to teach 86 year old Judith, who's practically your aunt at this point, why her double verification won't work. "Hand me that passbook, Judith"*)

Culture is the bridge between those realities. It's the difference between 'a few people are good at AI' and 'we have a shared way of working' (that's making our team exponentially impactful).

What Culture Actually Means in an AI Context

Culture isn't the values poster in the lobby. It's not the forced screen saver that changes every 3.7 days to reflect a calendar of events an influencer would be proud of. (*Though, bless whoever approved that budget.*) Culture is the lived system. It's what people do when the meeting ends and the deadline remains.

In an AI context, culture becomes the answer to a set of very practical questions.

When is it normal to use AI?

When is it not?

What's considered responsible?

What's considered sloppy?

What gets praised?

What gets punished?

What gets quietly tolerated?

If those answers are vague, people fill in the blanks themselves. They follow the loudest voice, the most anxious voice, or the voice of speed. None of those are inherently bad. But they are rarely aligned. That's how you get fragmented adoption: pockets of excellence, pockets of fear, and a general sense that nobody knows what the 'right way' is.

Chris McMartin, Business Banking National Lead, The Scotiabank Women Initiative, gave me one of the sharpest examples of cutting through that ambiguity. Chris is the kind of person who walks into a room full of entrepreneurs and radiates hype-person. Her only job is to shout you out. *(Her Instagram handle is literally 'hype boss'. Commitment to a brand, people. It's in the details.)* Beneath the energy she brings a razor-sharp read on how people actually behave.

When she talks about introducing AI to teams, her first question is disarmingly simple: *'What's the task that sucks the most? What's the task that the whole team would be happy to never do again?'*

And then she added the crucial second layer: *'Make it psychologically safe for them to tell you.'* Because too often, leaders ask questions to which they've already decided the answer. And people can sense that. *'Do it anonymously if you have to. Put it in a box. Tell me the one job you hate. It doesn't matter who it came from.'*

Then solve it. That's how you build buy-in. Not just with a keynote. With the removal of something that was making everyone miserable.

A strong AI culture does two things at once. It keeps learning alive. And it keeps risk contained. That balance is the work.

Framework: The Culture OS (6 Pillars)

The framework I offer up to leaders is designed to be simple enough to use in a leadership meeting and specific enough to guide action.

1. Playgrounds and Guardrails

2. Psychological Safety

3. Transparency as a Default

4. Quality, Voice, and Accountability

5. Access and Inclusion

6. Mentorship That Scales

You don't need perfection in all six. You do need intention. Whatever you don't define will be defined for you, by accident, by rumour, or by the path of least resistance.

Pillar 1: Playgrounds and Guardrails

Every meaningful change requires experimentation. That's how people learn. That's how innovation happens. But experimentation without boundaries becomes chaos. And chaos triggers the backlash that kills adoption.

Leaders tend to swing between two extremes. Wild West experimentation where anything goes. Or heavy documentation that reads like a scolding essay nobody asked for.

Neither works.

A healthy AI culture is pro-experimentation AND pro-safety at the same time. The language matters enormously here. When rules are framed as punishment, people hide. When rules are framed as enablement, people engage.

(We talked about this in Chapter 6 with Shona Boyd's guardrails framework. The three lines: never allowed, allowed with caution, safe by default. That's the foundation. Now we're talking about the CULTURE that makes people actually follow those lines instead of routing around them.)

If your organization has no legitimate place to play, people will still play. It will just be private, inconsistent, and harder to learn from. That's how shadow AI becomes normal without anyone meaning for it to.

The goal of guardrails is confidence. People plug in and support the mission when they know the boundaries.

Pillar 2: Psychological Safety

If you want people to share experiments, you need to make it safe to be imperfect.

AI triggers fear in ways many leaders underestimate. Some people fear being replaced. Others fear looking foolish. Some fear making a mistake that becomes public. And even confident leaders can feel the quiet pressure of *'I'm supposed to already understand this.'*

(If you've read Chapter 3 on the literacy divide, you know the shame gap is real and it runs deep.)

Chris McMartin named a dynamic that hit hard. She works extensively with women entrepreneurs, many of whom carry unease and shame around using AI. She told me about a time she forgot to change something in a LinkedIn post that identified it as AI-generated. Someone reached out, with concerned allyship, alerting Chris to the AI tell. *'It looks like AI did it.'*

Chris's response? *'AI did do it. I thought everyone knew. I didn't instantly get better at grammar.'*

And then she said the thing that should make every leader pause: *'I don't know any men who apologize for finding ways to do things better.'*

That sentence should be uncomfortable. It should also make you think about who in your organization feels safe admitting they use AI and who doesn't. Because safety is not evenly distributed. It never has been.

Safety is not coddling. It's clarity plus respect. It's leaders making it normal to say, 'I'm learning this too', and then BEHAVING in a way that proves it. It's responding to early mistakes with curiosity and suggestion, not correction and humiliation.

When people can speak early, you can steer early. When people stay quiet, you find out late. And late is expensive.

Pillar 3: Transparency as a Default

We are living in what folx call a trust recession.

People are wary.

Employees are wary.

Customers are wary.

In a world where it's harder to tell what's real, trust becomes a scarce resource.

This is where organizations make a critical mistake. They try to create trust by pretending nothing risky is happening. They assume that if they don't talk about AI use, AI use will remain contained.

It won't.

A healthy culture makes AI use visible without making it punishable. That's the nuance. If the only outcome of honesty is discipline, you'll get secrecy. If honesty is met with support and clearer guardrails, you'll get visibility.

Transparency turns scattered experiments into shared learning. It also gives leaders what they actually need: a view of reality, so governance is based on what IS happening rather than what you wish were happening.

The 'No AI' Policy Problem

I need to name this because I hear it more than you'd think.

'We have a blanket No AI policy.' (This is still common in 2026 when this book was published. Might not be such an issue if you're reading this several years later. But worth a read to see where we were.)

The intention is usually safety. The outcome is usually the opposite.

Here's why. People still have targets. Clients still expect speed. Teams still have more work than time. When AI becomes the easiest way to summarize notes, draft a first pass, or untangle a messy brief, the work doesn't stop because policy exists. It reroutes. Quietly.

So yes. Secret GPTs happen. Personal accounts happen. Browser tabs happen.

A mature culture doesn't pretend this away. It acknowledges the behaviour and brings it into the light. With structure, not shame. That means offering a safe sandbox, naming clear guardrails, and building a norm where it's okay to say 'I used AI here' the way it's okay to say 'I used a spreadsheet'.

If you push AI use into the shadows, you lose visibility. And when you lose visibility, you lose the ability to protect quality, privacy, and trust.

Pillar 4: Quality, Voice, and Accountability

AI can draft. Humans are accountable.

That sentence should sit near the centre of your culture. Because when output quality drops, trust drops. When trust drops, adoption stalls. And when adoption stalls, AI becomes a punchline rather than a capability.

Your organization needs a shared definition of 'done' for AI-assisted work. Not because you want to slow people down. Because you want to stop paying the hidden tax of rework.

There's also a brand dimension here. AI has a way of making things sound smooth and generic at the same time. If your organization values voice, nuance, and precision *(and you should)*, your culture must treat those as non-negotiable. Otherwise you'll produce work that's efficient and forgettable. And your customers WILL feel it.

Helen Patterson made a point here that applies to organizations of every size. She's been working with a creative company where people literally sketch by hand. *'This artistic ability, you don't want to lose that,'* she said. *'But then where can you create efficiencies?'* The answer isn't everywhere. It's specific. And knowing where quality and voice are non-negotiable versus where AI can handle the grunt work? That's a cultural decision, not a technical one.

Accountability is the final layer. If something goes wrong (facts wrong, tone off, sensitive information mishandled), your organization needs clarity about responsibility. Not to create scapegoats. To create seriousness. When accountability is vague, people either become reckless or frozen. Neither supports adoption.

Bad Tools Create Security Risks

Quick sidebar. If you don't provide enterprise-level tools that actually work, your people will find support elsewhere. When the official tools are clunky, blocked, or inferior, the job still needs to get done. So the workaround emerges: personal accounts, free versions, 'just this once' copy-pasting, and a quiet hope that nobody asks too many questions. It's what humans do when they're trapped between expectations and inadequate equipment.

This is why security and procurement can't treat AI as a moral debate. It's an infrastructure decision. Bad tools create shadow AI. Shadow AI creates unpredictable data handling. And unpredictable data handling is how small risks become big incidents.

The fix is a practical pathway. Give people tools that are safe AND usable, define clear guardrails in plain language, and train teams on what belongs in a system and what does not. If you want responsible behaviour at scale, you have to make the responsible path the EASIEST path. The subtext here is that all these tool licenses are going to cost money. Are organizations fully prepared for that?

Pillar 5: Access and Inclusion

Here's an uncomfortable question. Who gets to play?

When only the sales team gets training, or only technical roles get access, you slow adoption and you amplify existing biases. The people who already have proximity to power get more leverage. The people who are already under-resourced get left behind. And then we act surprised when the AI literacy divide looks a lot like every other divide we already have.

Heather Cannings, lead at StrikeUP Canada, pointed this out. She described the reality of many women, both entrepreneurs and mid-level employees, learning AI at 10 PM on the couch. Kids are in bed. The job is logged off. The dishes are done. I mean, how clear ARE our minds at this point?? The 10 PM problem is an access issue. It's a time poverty issue. It's the same literacy divide from Chapter 3, wearing different clothes.

Chris McMartin frames this as a leadership challenge: *'Don't leave it till 10 o'clock at night on the couch. Prioritize your learning. It should be as important as any certification. 10 AM on Mondays. Whatever it is. Because your development is important.'*

Sustainable adoption requires a shared floor of capability. If you let the literacy divide grow, you'll pay for it later in bottlenecks, resentment, and uneven quality.

If your culture treats learning as a personal hobby, AI adoption will remain a personal hobby. If your culture treats learning as part of work, AI adoption becomes part of work.

Pillar 6: Mentorship That Scales

Many organizations respond to AI by naming AI champions. That can work. It can also backfire spectacularly.

If champions become unpaid help desks, you'll burn out your best people. You'll create a hero system where one or two 'AI people' carry the organization while everyone else stays dependent. Adoption becomes fragile because it lives in a few brains instead of in shared workflows.

Helen Patterson brought a rich perspective here, because mentorship is literally her life's work. She's launched an initiative called One Million Mentor Moments, and her core belief stopped me in my tracks. '*Mentoring can just be one conversation*,' she said. '*You walk by someone at the water cooler and say, how are things going? What are you working on? You could solve a challenge right there in just one conversation.*'

And here's where Melissa Penton's framing from Chapter 6 comes back. Remember her insistence on experiential learning? '*This is not a technology that you can sit and talk about theoretically*,' she said. '*People need to learn by experience*.' Mentorship at scale is how you create that experiential learning without burning out the people leading it.

Mentorship means clear expectations about what champions do and don't do, and protection for their time. It means office hours, playbooks, templates, and clear pathways for others to level up. Champions are multipliers, not saviours.

Distributed learning is how culture becomes stable. Not through hero worship. Through systems.

Different Learners, Different Needs

One reason culture matters so much is that people adopt differently. If your culture rewards only one style (speed, caution, experimentation, or control), you will lose the other three. And then adoption becomes lopsided. You either have chaos without standards, or standards without energy.

A healthy culture gives each type of learner a legitimate role. It treats curiosity as valuable, caution as valuable, execution as valuable, and system-building as valuable.

The Power of Community

Chris McMartin made an observation about women entrepreneurs that applies here: *'I go into a room at a conference filled with women entrepreneurs, and there's five women over here that all do the same thing. Competitors. And there's no ounce of competition at the table. They're all chatting about, how'd you do that? And all of a sudden they're forming monthly calls.'*

She called it genius.

I call it the missing ingredient in most AI adoption strategies.

'Let's not compete with AI. Let's not compete with each other. Let's figure out how to make it a superpower together.'

Communities of practice are vastly underrated infrastructure. If you want adoption to spread, you need networks where people share what's working, troubleshoot what's not, and normalize the fact that everyone is figuring this out in real time.

Inside organizations, this looks like the show-and-tells and office hours we've been talking about. Outside organizations (for the founders and small business owners reading this), it looks like peer groups, masterminds, and the kind of collaborative spaces where competition takes a back seat to collective learning.

And a relevant plug here - this is exactly why I built AI Power Circle (AIPC). I created this AI implementation mastermind for small business owners and entrepreneurs who are looking for executive-level AI strategy and implementation for their growing teams. We meet on a loop. We share what's working. We troubleshoot what's not. We normalize the mess.

Meet Leigh Mitchell. She's a member inside of AI Power Circle and a great example of what this looks like in practice. Leigh is the Chief ChangeMaker behind Women in Biz Network and host of the ChangeMaker Leader Podcast. She's based in Toronto, she's a Forbes Impact Top 10 recipient, a Women of Microsoft award winner, and she teaches at York University and University of Guelph-Humber. She's built something called the Own Your Imprint™ framework, which helps leaders figure out their personal brand and then use AI to amplify it without losing the thing that makes them THEM. *(If that isn't impressive, I don't know what is. She's also a wonderful human.)*

When she joined AIPC, she was experimenting. Curious, capable, but doing most of it alone. Inside the community, she went from early tinkering to building full websites and workflows with tools like Lovable, Claude Cowork, Perplexity, and Comet, integrating AI across her marketing stack, and developing strong, informed perspectives on ethical AI use that she now shares across her considerable network and her students. She didn't just learn. She became someone who teaches others about AI. That's what community does. It turns one person's curiosity into a whole network's capability.

Since joining, Leigh tells me she feels less alone in this. And honestly, our friendship has grown through it too. She's shown up at our training sessions, helped at in-person AI events, and brought teaching ideas and resources back into the community that have made all of us sharper. She's also taken what she's learning in AIPC straight into her classrooms, helping her students build the AI literacy skills that are going to matter more than anything on their resumes in a few years.

That's the ripple effect of community. One person joins. They learn. They teach. They share. And the whole network levels up.

If that sounds like something you need in your life, scan the QR code below to learn more.

Three Patterns That Sabotage Adoption

Every organization has predictable ways of undermining itself. In AI adoption, three failure modes show up often. I've named them before in pieces throughout this book. Here they are together.

1. The Compliance-Only Trap.
This is the culture of 'don't'. Don't use external tools. Don't paste information. Don't experiment. Don't talk about it. It feels safe. It creates hiding. People still need to do the work. So they route around restrictions. They use personal tools. They stop sharing. Leaders lose visibility. Risk increases rather than decreases.

If you want safety, teach safe practice. If you want transparency, don't punish honesty.

2. Hero Culture.
One or two AI geniuses carry the organization. They build the prompts, answer every question, fix every workflow, become the unofficial help desk. It looks efficient at first. Then it breaks. Nothing scales. Champions burn out. Everyone else stays dependent. Adoption becomes fragile because it lives in people, not in systems.

3. Innovation Theatre.
Endless demos. Buzzwords. Shiny experiments that never change a workflow. It looks exciting. It photographs well. It can even win internal applause. But if it doesn't solve a problem, reduce rework, or improve a measurable outcome, it's less adoption and more entertainment.

The antidote: tie experimentation to real work. Graduate what works into standard practice. Kill what doesn't. *(The flywheel from Chapter 7 is designed for exactly this.)*

Design a Purposeful AI Culture

Culture can feel abstract until you give it shape. The goal here is to have a clear set of defaults that people can follow when they're busy and tired and under pressure.

Name your principles. Keep them plain. Keep them repeatable. You want principles people can actually remember when they're exhausted at 4 PM on a Thursday. 'We are pro-experimentation and pro-safety.' 'AI can draft; humans are accountable.' 'We surface risks early.' 'We value quality and voice.' These are decision filters.

Build rituals that make learning visible. Rituals reduce mental fatigue because they remove the need to decide, each week, whether (and where) learning fits. A show-and-tell every second Wednesday (for example) is effective. It tells the organization: this matters enough to get a permanent place on the calendar.

Align recognition with the behaviours you want. If you want people to improve workflows, recognize workflow improvement. Otherwise, the hard work of documenting, training, and refining becomes invisible labour. Even a small acknowledgement (naming a workflow improvement in a team meeting) signals that this work counts. A stronger signal is weaving AI literacy into performance conversations as a shared expectation.

Communicate like a human. Leaders set the emotional tone. If leaders only share wins, teams learn to hide failures. If leaders share what failed and what they learned, experimentation becomes safer and more honest.

These moves sound simple. They are. They are also not easy, because they require discipline and consistency. Sound familiar?

Culture Wraps Around the Flywheel

In Chapter 7, we built the flywheel: audit, train, build workflows, measure ROI, repeat.

Culture is the ring around that flywheel. Without it, the flywheel becomes a series of disconnected initiatives. With it, the flywheel becomes a habit. And habits are what create sustainability.

So when someone asks, *'Can we roll this out and be done by September?'* you can answer with a better question.

Can our culture support it?

And if not, what needs to change first?

Because culture determines whether people share learning, surface risks, protect quality, and repeat what works. Or whether they hide, drift, and quietly abandon.

AI is the app.

Culture is the operating system.

Update the OS.

The apps will run better.

CHAPTER 9

Buy / Build / Bolt-On

A leader's decision guide for turning AI from novelty into useful infrastructure.

Most leaders I meet are short on clarity when it comes to AI. They feel the ground moving. They feel the pressure to do something. And so the questions arrive in a rush, usually in the same breath: Should we build agents? Should we buy a tool? How good or bad is Copilot - because it's already in the stack?

These questions often sound strategic. They can even feel responsible. But underneath them is an assumption that keeps organizations stuck.

The assumption is that this is an all-or-nothing decision.

One big swing. One big bet. One giant agent that replaces whole departments and turns your operations into a frictionless machine.

That story is neat. It also collapses the moment it touches real work.

Because AI is not one thing.

It is a new layer of capability that can be applied in a thousand small places. If you want results you can trust, you don't need one monolith. You need a swarm of smaller tools, tuned to repeatable tasks, supported by guardrails, and improved over time.

Here I will help you think about what to buy, what to build, and what to bolt on. *(If you've been building from Chapter 7's flywheel, this is Pillar 3 in action. We're getting specific.)*

RPA for the Mind

A useful frame, especially if your team is tired of hype, is this: AI is Robotic Process Automation (RPA) for the human brain.

RPA is what happened in warehouses and logistics. At one point, humans did almost every step of the picking and packing process. As automation matured, robots took over the repeatable steps. Humans stayed focused on exceptions, judgement, and complex decisions.

AI is doing something similar in knowledge work. It takes over the mental drudgery: first drafts, formatting, summarizing, sorting, comparing, drafting variations, pulling patterns out of messy notes.

The goal is to free humans from robot work.

Suzanne Huber, who joined us in Chapter 6, summed this up in the most memorable way drawn from her sister's turn of phrase *'use your robot arms.'*

Robot arms. That's it. AI is an extension of your expertise. You're still the driver. You still need to know the difference between good and bad output. But with robot arms, you can do more, reach further, and save your actual brain for the parts that need a human brain.

The Queen Bee Strategy

One of the funnest mental models I've found is what Jason Dea called the Queen Bee AI strategy. You'll remember it from Chapter 2.

You are the Queen Bee.

AI is the swarm.

Nobody needs one giant bee. You need lots of little worker bees doing specific jobs: drafting, formatting, summarizing, checking, comparing, outlining, tagging, translating. All under your direction.

This matters because the super agent myth makes leaders do the wrong thing first. It makes them invest heavily before they understand their own work.

A swarm strategy does the opposite. It forces you to get specific. Build capability gradually. Keep humans in control.

The First Rule: Map the Workflow Before You Touch the Tools

Before you buy anything. Before you debate vendors, licences, models, or agents. You need to answer a plain question: **What, exactly, are we trying to improve?**

Not 'Marketing'

Not 'Sales enablement'

Not 'Operations'

Those are macro answers. They feel strategic, but they are too broad to automate. They're like saying, *'We should optimize the kitchen.'* Okay, great. The toaster? The pantry layout? The dishwasher schedule? WHICH PART?

A real answer sounds like: *'Turn messy meeting notes into a client-ready summary.'* Or: *'Draft a complex proposal from scattered inputs.'* Or: *'Route inbound requests to the right people with consistent language.'* Or: *'Pull metrics, spot patterns, and write a short insight brief.'*

Go deep, not broad.

Kirsten Schmidtke, the sales leadership consultant who joined us in Chapter 5, explains this well. She's seen organizations rush to AI for scale and then wonder why adoption stalled. Her diagnosis was simple: *'When we don't have clarity behind what it is we're building and why we're building it, AI can't help us with the how.'*

And then she named the risk of skipping this step: *'AI can actually create more work for us'* if we haven't first decided what to leave out and what to focus on. Clarity first. Tools second. *'It really requires you to know what you don't want the team focused on and what you do want the team focused on.'*

This isn't complicated. But it is skipped almost universally in the rush to 'do AI'.

The Unsexy List (Your Most Powerful AI Tool)

This is the most powerful AI tool in the room: a handwritten list.

Write the job as a 10-step chain. Use simple verbs.

I open. I check. I find. I copy. I rewrite. I compare. I ask someone. I format. I send. I follow up.

Your list will be messier than this. That's fine. The point is clarity.

If you can't list the steps, you can't automate them.
Not reliably. Not safely. Not in a way you'll trust.

And if you skip this step, AI becomes what it often becomes in modern teams: an expensive guessing game.

The Three Options Framework

Once you have a workflow mapped, the options become much simpler.

Option 1: Buy

You purchase an off-the-shelf solution that works largely as-is.

You buy when the job is standard. Summaries. Search. Analytics. Meeting notes. Transcript cleanup. Basic drafting support.

Buying is often the right move when you need reliability, enterprise support, and you do not want to maintain anything yourself.

A note-taker is a great 'buy' example. So is a reputable analytics or search tool. So is a specialized compliance-aligned solution when the risk profile is high. Buying frees your team from reinventing the wheel.

(And if you're thinking about enterprise-level buy decisions, remember the data and security conversation from Chapter 6. Shona Boyd was crystal clear: enterprise licences matter. Personal accounts and random subscriptions are not the same thing.)

Option 2: Bolt-On

You use AI features inside existing tools you already have.

Think: Copilot inside Microsoft 365. Gemini features inside Google Workspace. Built-in AI inside your CRM, ticketing system, or project management tool.

Bolt-on is underrated because it is fast, cheaper, and easier to change. It often has better permissioning and governance than random subscriptions spread across a team.

Bolt-on is not always best-in-class.

But it is often good enough to start the wheel.

This is how many teams should begin because it's realistic. It reduces shadow AI by making the safe path easier than the unofficial path.

And it helps you learn what you actually need before you spend time and money on custom work.

Option 3: Build

You create something custom using APIs, custom applications, or integrated model workflows.

Build is high effort and high reward.

It is also high responsibility.

You build when the workflow is your differentiator. Your moat. The thing that makes your business model work better than the competition. If your proprietary process or data is your advantage, custom builds can become strategic.

If the workflow is NOT your advantage, building is often an ego project with a maintenance bill.

Build is a commitment.
If you build something custom, you are building a living system. It needs monitoring. Evaluation. Feedback loops. Maintenance. Human review. A clear owner. A cadence. If you don't have the operating maturity to run it, you're building a liability, not an advantage.

The Six Levels of Personalized Tools

A lot of leaders get stuck because they think in binaries: build an agent or don't.

In reality, there are levels between 'chatting with a model' and 'building a custom platform'. Here is a ladder you can climb without breaking anything.

Level 1: Better prompts. One-off help. You ask a question, you get an answer. This is where most people start.

Level 2: Prompt libraries. Repeatable help. Templates that other people can grab without rethinking the thing from scratch.

Level 3: Custom GPTs, Gems, Projects, Skills. Consistent behaviour. The tool knows your context, your voice, your constraints.

Level 4: Workflow automation. Handoffs between steps. Now you're chaining tasks together.

Level 5: Integrated systems. Data, permissions, governance. Enterprise-level setup.

Level 6: Custom builds. Strategic differentiation. You've got the resources and the reason.

This ladder should feel a bit like a relief because it means you don't have to jump from zero to agentic transformation. You can evolve. You can test. You can build competence as you go.

And that, in practice, is how sustainable adoption happens.

What Building Actually Looks Like (in the Wild)

Let me introduce two people who live on this ladder every day.

Dr. Jim Kanichirayil is the founder of Cascading Leadership, a GTM agency for early-stage founders. He's the kind of person who opens a conversation with a Dr. Evil impression and then casually drops the most practical advice you'll have heard all week. He lives in ChatGPT and has built custom GPTs for everything from cold email generation to content analysis to product launches.

Andrew Jenkins runs Volterra Digital, a social media agency based in Toronto. He was my instructor at the University of Toronto in the School of Continuing Studies where I studied digital strategy. Andrew works across multiple platforms, talks to the machine like a colleague, and has one of the sharpest eyes for where AI helps and where it creates risk.

The two of them joined me for a conversation about whether you should build custom tools or just get better at prompting. The answer, as with most good advice, was 'it depends'. But the details are gold.

Dr. Jim's Approach: Role, Task, Output

Dr. Jim's framework for building a custom GPT is disarmingly simple. *'The simplest framework I use to get started,'* he told me, *'is role, task, and output. What is the role that you want the tool to play? What's the task that you want it to accomplish? And what should the output look like?'*

That's it. That's the starter. Role. Task. Output.

But then he added the step that separates good from great: *'Ask it the question: what else do you need to properly execute this task and have the output be highly reflective of my voice?'* Because that's where most people stop too early. They get decent output and call it done. Dr. Jim pushes until the output actually sounds like him.

He explained why he moved from prompting to custom GPTs in the first place: *'I started trying to do that through just pure prompting, but the prompts would lose focus over time. And I found that projects did the same thing. So when I started noticing consistent bleed-out, I built a GPT for that particular task.'*

Cold email generation. Content analysis engines. Product launch playbooks. Each one built for an isolated, repeatable task. Each one trained on his voice, his method, his context. *(Are you seeing Jason Dea's swarm of bees analogy in action here??)*

And here's the part that makes Dr. Jim's approach different from many - he maintains his GPTs. When they start drifting (and they will), he goes back into the configuration and asks the tool to do a root cause analysis on itself. *'What are the root causes for why this is happening? And what do I need to add into the training material so that it avoids producing this sort of output?'*

That's not building once and walking away. That's operating a system. (Which is why 'build' belongs higher on the ladder than most people want it to.)

The Chain Rule

Dr. Jim described something that should be required reading for anyone thinking about agents. He chains his tools together. Not as one massive system. As a series of connected small tools.

'You have a GPT that's built on your voice to produce scripts', he explained. *'You produce the content that follows the script after you've refined it. Then you measure how well this script is landing, and you use an analysis GPT to close the loop. That defines what your next batch of content looks like.'*

Read that again. He has a content GPT, a production process with human refinement, and an analysis GPT that feeds back into the next cycle. That's a chain. That's a system. And at every link, there's a human making decisions.

If you do build, don't lust after super agents. Chain things. Start with one small link. Improve it. Measure it. Add the next link. Keep humans reviewing outputs. Keep feedback loops alive.

A system of small connected tools will outperform a massive one-time build almost every time, because it can evolve without collapsing.

Automation Versus Autopilot

Automation is scaling.

Autopilot is abdication.

Automation means you use AI to remove drudgery while humans stay accountable. Autopilot means you let AI outputs go live without review. That's where quality collapses. That's where brand drift grows. That's where risk raucously blooms.

Andrew Jenkins drew this line sharply. *'Automation to help scale, to do more with less, to make existing resources more productive? Great',* he said. *'Autopilot? Too many risks there.'*

He gave a specific example that made me wince: automated outreach on LinkedIn. *'I don't buy from a bot. Why would I think that a bot representing me is going to do my sales job?'*

Kirsten Schmidtke backed this up from the sales side. She named what's happening in buyer psychology right now: *'We are in a trust recession. Buyers are much more skeptical. Much more confused. And a confused buyer does not buy.'* AI has contributed to that erosion of trust when it's used carelessly. When messages don't connect, when there's no intention behind the outreach, people spot it instantly. *'We can call it out right away.'*

And then Dr. Jim Kanichirayil completed the picture from the content side. He sees people treating AI output as a final product everywhere. *'No matter how well you've trained it, whatever you get is probably a 60 or 70 percent draft',* he said. *'People post those as good enough without asking themselves: does this sound like me? Is this something I would say?'*

The result? Content that has *'unnatural pivots, hyperbole, and a tendency to be too cliche.'* The telltale signs of someone running with a draft instead of polishing it to have their own voice.

(And we don't just mean the odd LinkedIn post here. We've seen massive consultancies sending off AI first drafts that got them in trouble and caused them to have to return mid-six figure sums in breach of contract.)

Garbage in, garbage out isn't just a meme or a software project management *mantra*.

It's a leadership issue.

If you want to build trust in AI, you need a non-negotiable norm - no output goes live without human review. Because humans are accountable.

Dr. Jim framed the distinction perfectly: *'A human in the lead approach versus a human in the loop approach.'* Human in the loop means you're checking a box. Human in the lead means you're actively steering. The second one is harder. The second one is also the only one that produces work you'd put your name on.

Decision Filters That Actually Work

Now that you have the workflow steps mapped, you can make the buy/build/bolt-on decision with far less drama.

Here are four filters I recommend leaders use.

Filter A: Repeatable or one-off?
If the task is repeatable and boring, you are in tool territory. Bolt-ons, automations, and small worker bees. If it's one-off and strategic, you

may need an assistant: a workhorse tool that supports thinking rather than replacing it.

Filter B: Where is the advantage?
Most of the time, the winners are not the people who invent the tech. They are the people who see how the tech changes their business model and use it to create advantage. If your advantage is how you apply the tech, buy or bolt-on is usually plenty. If your advantage is the system itself (proprietary method, unique data, differentiated experience), then building may be worth it.

Filter C: Data and risk.
This one is non-negotiable. If the workflow touches customer PII *(personal identifier information - think of it like the AI version of your IP address-ish)*, proprietary metrics, internal performance data, or confidential information, you must use enterprise-grade tools and governed environments. Never paste sensitive data into a public model. Not even 'just once'. Not even 'but we stripped the names'.

Filter D: Operating maturity.
This is where agentic dreams go to die. If you build something custom, you are building a living system. It needs monitoring, evaluation, feedback loops, maintenance, human review, a clear owner, and a cadence. If you don't have the operating maturity to run it, you are building a future problem.

Kirsten named this dynamic in the sales context. One of her clients described their approach as *'AI forward'* rather than 'AI first.' *'It wasn't: we need to push AI for the sake of AI,'* Kirsten explained. *'It's: we want to be forward-thinking and intentional about where it comes into our processes, how it augments the sales team. It's not about removing humans from selling.'*

AI forward. Not AI first. That's a decision filter in a sentence.

Your Move - the Circle Exercise

Go back to your unsexy list. The 10-step workflow.

Circle the friction points. The annoying parts. The repeated parts. The chaotic parts.

Now label each circled step with one letter:

R = Repeatable

J = Judgement-heavy

D = Data-sensitive

Then scan.

If you see mostly **R**, start with bolt-on. Use the tools you already have. Make small, consistent helpers. Automate handoffs.

If you see mostly **D**, start with enterprise buy or bolt-on. Governed access. Permissioning. Guardrails. No improvising.

If you see mostly **J**, keep humans in the lead. Buy tools that assist and speed up, but don't pretend automation replaces judgement.

If you see a mix of **R + D** and the workflow is your differentiator, that's the moment to consider building. Only if you can support it properly.

The Decision Sentence

Fill this in:

'For this workflow, we will [Buy / Build / Bolt-On] because the biggest constraint is [Time / Security / Repeatability].'

Write one sentence per workflow.

If you can't write the sentence, you don't understand the work yet. Go back to the steps.

That sentence is your strategy.

Everything else is procurement.

This, and all the other mini exercises in this book are in one easy place for you to access. Scan the QR code below or visit: https://wearenorthlightai.com/swan-dive-backwards

The Real Goal is White Space

There is a reason I keep returning to this: the point of these decisions is not AI everywhere. Instead it is preserving white space for your people.

Keep the judgement and creativity. Automate the noise.

If you can protect 60% of your people's capacity for thinking and relationship work by removing 40% of repetitive drudgery, you get better decisions. Better quality. Better care. Better work.

That's a competitive advantage that will show up in what your team can hold.

(We talked about this in Chapter 7 as the flywheel's purpose. And in Chapter 8 as the reason culture matters. The tools conversation from this chapter is HOW you protect that white space. The culture conversation is WHY people trust you enough to use the tools well on your behalf.)

CHAPTER 10

Building Your Beehive

You mapped the work. You made the decision.
Now let's build the damn thing.

There is a specific kind of stalling that happens after clarity arrives.

You did the work from Chapter 9. You mapped the workflow. You labelled the friction. You wrote the decision sentence. You know whether you're buying, building, or bolting on.

And then nothing happens. Because the gap between deciding and doing feels like a canyon. On one side is the strategy. On the other side is a blinking cursor and the sinking feeling that you may be in over your ears.

I know this feeling. I have LIVED this feeling.

(More than once, if we're being honest.)

So this chapter is about the build. The actual, roll-up-your-sleeves, open-the-tool, make-the-thing part.

Because a strategy that lives in a Google Doc is not a strategy.

It's a wish.

And wishes don't scale.

What a beehive actually looks like (not the metaphor, the reality)

We've been talking about the beehive since Jason Dea first handed me that image back in Chapter 2. A swarm of worker bees. You're the queen. Each bee has a specific job.

Beautiful metaphor.

But metaphors don't ship.

So let's look at what Jason actually built.

He has AI trained on his voice and style. But here's the part most people miss: it's not *one* AI. It's a series of mini AIs, each with a different job. One is specifically trained to help him write social media content. Same background context as the others. Same voice. Different task.

Another one's entire purpose is creating PowerPoint presentations. It knows his stylistic preferences, his tone, his colour scheme. *(Yes, colour scheme. Because brand specifics are not intuitive with many AI tools.)*

A third one writes requirements documentation for his product management work.

Say it with me... Same background. Same voice. Different function. That's a beehive. Not one mega-bot that does *everything*. A fleet of small, focused helpers that each do one thing well.

And when you look at it that way, the whole thing gets less intimidating.

Pick your workhorse first

Before you build a single bee, you need a hive. Shona Boyd's advice is to pick the workhorse first. A ChatGPT or a Claude, depending on your usage. Set it up at the enterprise level. Because that allows you to actually use your data and connect it to your internal data points, which makes the answers richer. And she stresses: *'It stays there in your instance.'*

The distinction between enterprise and personal is the difference between your data going into the training soup and your data staying where it belongs.

Your goal at this stage is not to find the perfect platform. What you're looking for instead is a safe default. Why? Because if you don't, your team will pick for you. And they'll pick whatever's fastest. Which is usually whatever's on their phone. Which is usually not enterprise-grade.

Shona Boyd gave me an example that many of us find so familiar that it may be blindness at this point but it should really make your eye twitch. She'd join meetings and some random AI note-taker would pop into the call. And everyone would look around like, whose is this? Until someone chimes, 'Oh, I was just trying something out.' She put it plainly: *'There's a lot more people doing it than you think.'*

(She used to work at a law firm, folx. She is not messing around about this.)

So step one of building your beehive is not exciting. It's not glamorous. It's choosing one workhorse, setting it up properly, and making it the easy path for your people.

Utility always wins. Your job is to make utility safe.

Train it like a team member

Allow me to re-introduce you to Gazzy Amin, because she'll change how you think about the building process. Gazzy is a business strategist and Founder of Sales Beyond Scripts. She focuses on working with women entrepreneurs. She's also one of those people who makes you feel like anything is possible while simultaneously making you accountable for actually doing it!

When Gazzy talks about AI, she doesn't talk about it like technology. She talks about it like a team member. And that shift in framing changes **everything**. She told me: *'AI is only as good as the training you give it, which is like any other team member. You have to train it to get it to the level that you want. And the more context and input, the better the output.'*

Gazzy brings you further into what that training looks like... Every podcast episode transcript goes in. Every masterclass she's done. Every event. Every workbook. Every sales conversation. She grabs the audio of real conversations and feeds the transcriptions to her AI so it learns how she actually talks.

And the result? *'She (Gazzy's AI) knows that I'm sassy. She's like, oh, you want me to give sassy or Gazzy CEO direct?' Because I just say it how it is.'*

I love that her AI has nicknames for her communication styles. That is PEAK personalization.

But here's the part that actually matters for your beehive. Gazzy doesn't just use AI for content. She told me that most people default to captions and emails, and that's the most obvious use. But it's one small way.

She uses it for financial audits. For business planning. For sales process documentation. She literally walked her AI through her entire sales process in real time. Every step. The Zoom transcription after the call. The payment through QuickBooks. The follow-up.

And then she asked it: *'What are some ways I could be automating? Which parts of this should I automate to make it a better client experience?'*

The AI came back with a twelve-step client onboarding system, complete with software recommendations she hadn't considered.

She said: *'I could have never thought of this on my own. I would have had to pay multiple people.'*

That's business architecture! And it started with one thing - giving the AI enough real context to actually be useful.

The 'feed it everything' rule

Gazzy Amins's approach exposes the single biggest mistake people make when building their first tools. They give them nothing to work with. They type a prompt. They get a generic answer. They decide AI 'doesn't work for my business'. They go back to doing everything manually.

The problem was never the technology.

The problem was data starvation.

You hired a team member and gave them zero onboarding. No context. No examples. No history. No voice samples. Then you got mad when they produced something that sounded like a stranger wrote it.

Of course it sounded like a stranger wrote it. To the AI, you ARE a stranger.

Fix that.

If you feel like your AI outputs are vague, Gazzy's advice is direct: *'It's because you haven't given it enough information.'*

Feed it your real voice. Your real examples. Your real process. Your real data. (Inside an enterprise tool, obvi. See the workhorse section above.)

Gazzy also said: *'If you're using (AI), just get smart on how you're using it, and train it better and learn how to stand out in an ocean of people who are only using it in a very specific way.'*

The builder thread: using AI to build your AI

Okay, here's a trick that most people don't know about yet. And it's one of the most powerful things I've learned in this entire process.

You don't have to write your AI instructions from scratch.

You can use AI to write them FOR you.

I know. It sounds like 'Inception'. It kind of is.

Here's how it works. I keep a separate thread (call it a builder thread or a system thread) that I've set up to think like a product architect.

I go back and forth with this thread to build out GPT and skills instructions.

When I describe a workflow from my own head, I'll give you maybe ten steps. Makes sense to me. But there are actually twenty-two steps, because my brain skips the obvious ones.

(Of COURSE you'd get a transcript immediately after recording. Of COURSE you'd upload it. Of COURSE you'd create an email from it. But I might not write those steps down because they feel like a given.)

The builder thread catches all of that. It thinks of the steps my brain glosses over.

And then it goes further. It asks: can we put a set of voice examples in the knowledge base? And I'll create a document (or have it create one) that captures the specific tone, the specific vocabulary, the specific do's and don'ts.

So the process is to brain dump your workflow to the builder thread (use voice notes for extra simplification). Let it expand and refine the instructions. Upload supporting documents as the knowledge base. Test. Adjust. Repeat.

You're essentially getting the machine to prompt itself.

The No-Build Alternative (or: what if you just talked to it?)

Okay. I need to present the counterargument to everything I just said. Because not everyone needs a builder thread. Not everyone needs a custom GPT or an artefact. Not everyone needs to architect a system with instructions and knowledge bases and guardrails.

Sometimes you just need to be really, REALLY good at talking to the machine.

Andrew Jenkins, who runs the social media agency Volterra Digital in Toronto, has an approach to AI that is the polar opposite of the build-it-from-scratch method. Andrew doesn't build a lot of custom tools. He doesn't tinker endlessly with configurations. He does something that sounds deceptively simple.

He has conversations.

Good ones.

As he put it: *"I put the chat in ChatGPT."*

Getting the machine to prompt itself

Here is what Andrew does that most people don't. He lets the AI tell HIM what it needs to know. Instead of walking in with a perfectly crafted prompt (which, let's be honest, most of us are not going to write), he opens with context and then asks the machine to figure out the next steps.

He gave me an example. When a new ChatGPT model dropped, he didn't go hunting for tutorials or prompt libraries. He literally just said: *"Given what you know about me, the company I run, and the clients that we serve, what are the top three to five things I should know about your capabilities as a new version, or where can you help me?"*

The AI gave him five areas where it could help. Then it offered to create a prompt library for those areas. Then it offered to build a workflow. *"Just that one initiation of a conversation, that one question posed to it, led to those multiple steps that it proactively was suggesting to me"*, Andrew said.

He didn't build the workflow. The machine built it for him. Because he asked the right opening question and then stayed in the conversation long enough for the machine to find its own path forward.

That is what I mean by getting the machine to prompt itself.

The "master prompt" (my favourite trick that nobody uses enough)
I want to give you a technique I use ALL the time that connects to what Andrew is doing. I call it "the master prompt" because it gives the machine a structured way to extract exactly what it needs from you before it starts working.

Here's how it works. Instead of trying to write the perfect brief (which, again, nobody does), you say something like this: *"Before you start, I want you to ask me up to 10 questions that will give you everything you need to do this task really well. Ask them all at once."*

That's the master prompt. Cap it at 10 questions so it doesn't become an endless discovery session. *(Trust me on the cap. Without it, some models will ask you 47 questions and you'll lose the will to live.)*

What happens next is genuinely useful. The machine comes back with a focused set of questions that cover the gaps IT identified. Things you wouldn't have thought to include. Things your brain skipped because they felt obvious. Things that are actually critical to the quality of what it's about to produce.

And here's the beautiful part. Many of the newer models already ask you two or three clarifying questions on their own. They've been built to do that. But two or three questions from the machine is a snack. Ten questions is a meal. And a well-fed AI produces dramatically better output than a hungry one.

(See what I did there? Full circle back to the data starvation problem from earlier in this chapter. Except this time, instead of you doing all the feeding, you're letting the machine tell you what it's hungry for.)

Context as fuel, not decoration

Andrew takes this further with how he thinks about source material. His philosophy is simple: give it everything. *"I'd rather err on the side of giving as much as I can"*, he told me, *"so that then I've got this well of information that I can have a conversation about, pose questions to, or ask the AI tool what's missing, what additional information do you need."*

What he is doing is running a continuous feedback loop between his context and the machine's appetite.

He does this with his book, for example. Andrew wrote ***"Social Media Marketing for Business"*** and he keeps the chapters in a project so he can come back to the material from different angles. One day he might brainstorm blog topics from it. Another day he might pull case studies for a LinkedIn post. He's not going chapter by chapter. He's using the source material holistically and letting the AI help him see connections across the whole thing.

"I'm just coming at it with, oh, today I want to talk to the book via AI about this subject", he said. *"And so I brainstorm with the AI about what we can do from the book."*

Talk to the book!!!

That surreal sentence captures exactly what this approach is. Not commanding. Not instructing. Conversing.

When to talk versus when to build

So now you might be thinking: wait, Susan, you just spent the first half of this chapter teaching me to build bees with instructions and knowledge bases and guardrails. Now you're telling me I can just... talk to it?

Yes. And also no.

Here's how to think about it.

If the task is REPEATABLE and you need CONSISTENT output every time *(the same kind of report, the same kind of email, the same kind of social post)*, build a bee. Give it rules. Give it a knowledge base. Make it a system. Because consistency requires structure, and structure requires a build.

But if the task is STRATEGIC or EXPLORATORY *(you're brainstorming, you're analyzing new information, you're trying to figure out an approach, you're working through something messy and complex)*, you probably don't need to build anything. You need Andrew's approach. A good opening question. A willingness to stay in the conversation. And the instinct to let the machine tell you what it needs.

The master prompt works beautifully here. You walk in with your messy context, you ask for ten questions, you answer them, and now the machine has a brief that's better than what most humans would write from scratch. No custom GPT required. No builder thread. No system architecture. Just a conversation between a curious human and a machine that's been given permission to be curious back.

Andrew and Dr. Jim *(who you'll remember from Chapter 9)* actually represent two ends of the same spectrum. Dr. Jim builds GPTs for repeatable tasks and asks the machine to do root cause analysis on itself when the output drifts. Andrew stays in conversations and asks the machine to optimize itself in real time. The principle is this - the machine already knows how to be better at its job. You just have to ask.

The one question that changes everything

If you take nothing else from Andrew's approach, take this.

After you've given the AI your context, your brief, your messy voice note, your brain dump, whatever it is, ask one more question before you let it start working: *"What else do you need from me to do this really well?"*

That question takes three seconds to type. Andrew and Dr Jim and I - all use it regularly. And it consistently produces better outcomes because it turns a one-way instruction into a two-way collaboration. You're letting it feed itself.

And that, folx, is its own kind of beehive. One that doesn't require a single thing to be built.

When your context is the product

Andrew Jenkins gave me a distinction I want you to hold onto, because it will save you from building the wrong thing.

Sometimes your work is a repeatable task. The same kind of output, over and over, with slightly different inputs. Monthly blog posts. Standard proposals. Client update emails. Weekly reports.

For that, you want a dedicated assistant. A GPT. A gem. A Claude Skill. An internal bot. Something that holds the rules, holds the style, holds the output constraints. You give it input, it gives you a draft. Same dance, every time.

But sometimes your work is a living body of knowledge. A book manuscript. A research archive. A product documentation library. A brand strategy that's been evolving for eighteen months. For that, you don't just need a bot. You need a *project*. A place where the context stays intact over time. Where you're not asking a tool to do a single job. You're asking it to think alongside an entire corpus.

Andrew described it as having access to a body of knowledge you can have a conversation with - especially if you use a tool like Notebook LM. He said he'd rather err on the side of giving as much context as possible, so that he's got this well of information to draw from.

This distinction matters because people build the wrong shape of tool all the time. They build a one-shot assistant when they need a project. (And the tool keeps forgetting context.) Or they dump everything into a project when they just need a simple, repeatable bot. (And the tool gets overwhelmed with irrelevant information.)

So before you build, ask: is this a task or a knowledge base?

Task? Build a bee.

Knowledge base? Build a project.

Different containers. Different strengths. Both useful. Neither is a substitute for the other.

The sprawl problem (or: when your hive gets overrun)

I need to talk about the other side of all this building enthusiasm, because it's a real risk that nobody wants to discuss at the strategy retreat.

Every SaaS platform now has an AI assistant bolted on.

Your CRM has one. Your email client has one. Your project management tool has one. Your analytics platform has one. Your note-taking app has one. That random tool you signed up for during the pandy and forgot to cancel? It has one too.

Which means your data, your drafts, your reasoning, and your prompts can end up scattered across dozens of little micro-bots that nobody governs.

Jason Dea calls this out as the next generation of shadow IT. He said: *'The previous generation of this problem, we called shadow IT. With SaaS, anybody could turn on a new service with just a credit card. And what emerged was this laundry list of tools that nobody knew about. The same thing is starting to happen with AI. And the blast radius is actually quite a bit larger, because many of these AIs are able to perform tasks autonomously, which SaaS historically wasn't really able to do.'*

Blast radius. Let that term sit with you for a second.

Shona Boyd sees it too. She told me: *'Every product I touch is like, hey, would you like? No. No, I don't. Sometimes I just want to scroll.'*

So how do you build a beehive without creating a swarm that's out of control? You orchestrate.

Jason Dea nailed this point. The root cause of both shadow IT and shadow AI is the same thing - a lack of clarity around the workflow itself and specifically the orchestration of the workflow.

Translation: if you don't know who's using what, on what data, for what purpose, connected to what else, you don't have a beehive.

You have a jar of bees you knocked over.

Very different energy.

The visibility fix

The answer to sprawl is not a ban. We covered that in Chapter 6. Bans don't work. People just go underground.

The answer is visibility.

A personalized tool that lives in one person's head is not a team asset. It's a personal superpower that leaves when they leave.

So once you've built your bees (even one or two), make them visible. Create a simple internal registry. Nothing fancy. A shared doc. A Notion page. A row in a spreadsheet. Whatever your team will actually use.

For each bee, capture five things:

Name: What do you call it? *(Gazzy Amin would approve of giving it a personality.)*

Purpose: What specific job does it do?

Who uses it: Is this a team tool or a personal one?

What data is safe: What can you feed it? What's off limits?

Where outputs get reviewed: Who checks the work before it ships?

That's it. Five lines. Per bee.

That tiny act of documentation transforms experiments into infrastructure. It turns a personal advantage into a team capability. And it gives leadership something they desperately need - a map of what's actually happening with AI in their organization.

Because right now, for most organizations, the honest answer to 'how is your team using AI?' is a shrug.

A registry replaces the shrug with a story.

(And the story usually makes a pretty compelling business case for what to invest in next.)

What this looks like at scale

I want to come back to Gazzy Amind for a moment because she said something super cool. She was describing how she launched her CEO Growth Plan intensive. A full product launch. Landing page. Facebook ads. Nine ad scripts. Email sequences. The works.

She did it in three and a half weeks. With a team of three people. All of them using AI.

She said: *'I didn't fire anybody, but we're all using AI to create this. Some companies, this would take them months.'*

And then she talked about what scaled because of this. *'There was a time where I could only onboard one or two clients at a time, because it would take so much creative energy. Now I could create twenty ads in a day, because I have my thinking partner.'*

The result? She can make more money. She can onboard more clients. She doesn't need three executive assistants. Her EA can do the work of three.

But here's the part I want you to catch.

She didn't start by buying a fancy platform.

She started by sitting with ChatGPT for six hours, going back and forth, refining nine ad scripts until they sounded like HER. Not like a bot. Not like a template. Like Gazzy.

That's the work.

That's always the work.

The tool amplified her creative energy. And it freed up capacity for the things that only she can do - coaching, connecting, showing up live, reading the room.

She's even told her EA: *'I want you to spend two hours a week learning how we can use AI to advance and scale the company.'*

Not 'your job is in danger'.

Not 'figure this out or else'.

'Spend two hours a week learning.'

That is leadership. That is how you build a culture where the beehive grows without chaos.

(If you're thinking this connects back to Chapter 8's conversation about culture being the operating system, you're absolutely right. It does.)

Your move: build your first bee in thirty minutes

Enough theory.

Grab a blank page. Set a timer. Thirty minutes.

Step 1: Name the micro-task

Not 'Marketing'. Not 'Sales'. Not 'Operations'.

Name the *micro-task*: *'Turn meeting notes into a client update email.'* Or *'Summarize this week's support tickets into a trend report.'* Or *'Draft a LinkedIn post from my podcast transcript.'*

One task. One bee. That's it.

Step 2: Write the Role, Task, Output

(You remember this from Chapter 9. Dr. Jim Kanichirayil's framework. Use it.)

Role: 'You are my client-facing account manager.'

Task: 'Turn these meeting notes into an email update for the client.'

Output: 'Include decisions, next steps, and dates. No fluff. Canadian spelling. Three paragraphs max.'

Then, as Dr. Jim taught us: ask it what else it needs to properly execute the task. Let the tool tell you what's missing.

Step 3: Add three guardrails

What must NEVER be included? (Internal pricing? Confidential names? Speculation?)

What must ALWAYS be verified? (Dates? Dollar amounts? Commitments?)

What tone is non-negotiable? (Warm but professional? Direct? Casual?)

Step 4: Test with three real examples

One easy one. (Clean notes, straightforward update.)

One messy one. (Rambling notes, unclear action items.)

One high-stakes one. (Sensitive content, important client.)

The messy one and the high-stakes one are where you'll learn the most. That's where the guardrails either hold or they don't.

Step 5: Write one sentence that defines success

'This bee saves twenty minutes per client update and reduces missed action items.'

Or: 'This bee produces a first draft that requires less than five minutes of editing.'

Or: 'This bee catches the follow-ups I always forget.'

One sentence. Measurable. Specific.

That sentence is your quality standard. It's also the thing you'll use to decide whether this bee earns a permanent spot in the hive or gets retired.

Congratulations. You just built a leadership artefact. Because you took invisible, repetitive work and turned it into something teachable. Something transferable. Something that doesn't live only in your head anymore.

That is what building a beehive actually looks like.

Not a moonshot. Not a transformation initiative. Not a six-month roadmap.

Thirty minutes and a blank page.

The point of building is not output. It's white space.

I know it's tempting to measure your beehive by volume. More drafts. More posts. More reports. More meetings summarized. More emails sent.

Resist that.

The point of a beehive is not to fill every hour with more productivity.

The point is to create space.

Space for your people to solve the hairy problems. Space to actually think. Space to have the human conversations that build trust and close deals and spark ideas.

Gazzy Amin called her AI a thinking partner. Not a replacement. A partner.

Jason Dea described it as a swarm of helpers that free up the queen bee to focus on what matters.

Shona Boyd insists on enterprise-grade tools because she knows the human work is too important to risk on sloppy data practices.

Different people. Different industries. Same conclusion.

Build your bees. Train them well. Make them visible. Keep humans accountable.

And use the time you get back to do the work that only you can do.

CHAPTER 11

AI Champions

From secret power users to supported guides.

You've seen it happen. You're in a meeting, and one person's work lands on the table with a kind of polish that feels almost unfair. Their draft is clean. Their thinking is structured. Their answers arrive in the room faster than the questions can fully form.

It's 'suspiciously quick'.

Not flashy. Not loud. Just ahead.

If you ask how they did it, they'll usually shrug. They'll say something like, 'Oh, I just played around.' They might name a tool casually, like it's no different than opening a spreadsheet.

But what they've actually done is more important than a tool choice.

They've quietly built a personal AI stack.

They swan dove backwards off the cliff.

And without meaning to, they've become your organization's informal R&D lab.

Every organization has these people.

Almost none recognize them properly.

And that is a mistake. Because power users left unsupported become exhausted or invisible. Or both.

What's actually happening (whether you designed it or not)

Inside your organization right now, your AI future is already being prototyped. Not by a consultant. Not by an AI task force. Not by the vendor who sold you the enterprise licence. By a handful of people who got curious and didn't wait for permission.

They're testing AI in real workflows, inside your approved stack (or not). They're figuring out what works and what breaks. They're learning to have conversations with machines in ways that actually produce useful output. And they're doing the awkward, messy part of learning that most people avoid.

These people are your research and development lab. Whether or not you realize it. Whether or not you've named them that.

And they're valuable for a reason that has nothing to do with technical skill. They understand context. They understand your organization's language. They care about getting the work done. That's WHY they made the tech work for them.

'Do we have AI power users?', I hear you ask. Yes, yes you do. The question to ask is: *'where are our AI power users, and what are we doing to support them?'*

Because if you ignore them, three things happen. One, they get tired of doing extra work with no support. Two, their knowledge stays trapped in their heads or their personal accounts. And three, your organization misses a chance to scale what's actually working.

This chapter is about doing the opposite.

Champions are a bridge.

When you support champions, something subtle shifts. AI becomes social. It gets a human face. And when AI has a human face that peers trust, adoption moves from mandatory to interesting. From compliance to curiosity. From isolated wins to shared progress.

Helen Patterson, who you met in Chapter 8, put it in a way that stuck with me. She's been studying mentorship cultures for years, and she made a connection that I think is the key to understanding champions. She told me: *'Organizations are creating these internal champions and those folks are helping other folks. And that's just mentorship.'*

I love that framing. Because 'AI champion program' sounds like a corporate initiative. Mentorship sounds like something humans do naturally when they care about each other.

That's what champions do at their best. They have a conversation. They show a colleague something useful. They remove the mystery. That is the bridge champions create. But only if you design the role well. Because there is a dark side.

The unpaid help desk problem (and why it ruins everything)

This is the quickest way to sabotage your future.

You identify your most capable AI users. You praise them publicly. And then, without changing anything else, you start routing everyone's questions to them.

Suddenly they're troubleshooting. They're running impromptu trainings. They're pulled into 'pilot projects' that are really just code words for more work on top of your already crazy days.

Your champion becomes tired.

And tired people don't keep experimenting. They stop sharing. They retreat back into private workflows. Sometimes into personal accounts. Sometimes into silence.

I know this happens because I have a bunch of senior nine-to-fivers in my circle, and many of them are AI early adopters. In their companies, they've been pulled to the front to be part of 'pilot projects'. And those are all just code words for more work, but unpaid this time. As one of them told me: *'If I knew this was going to become my second job, I might have kept my mouth shut.'*

That should haunt every leader reading this chapter. Because that person has lost faith that their organization will support them properly. *(Would you be surprised if I told you they left shortly afterwards to work elsewhere?)* If you don't adjust expectations, your best champions will burn out and go back into hiding *(or leave)*. And that doesn't help them. It doesn't help you. It doesn't help anyone *(except maybe your competitors)*.

The first skill is finding them

You can't support what you can't see. The problem is that many organizations look for champions the wrong way. They ask a yes-or-no question: *'Are you using AI workflows?'* That question produces polite, low-signal answers. It also triggers fear in people who aren't sure what's allowed.

(If you did the audit work from Chapter 5, you're ahead of the game here. If you didn't, this is your second chance.)

A better question is a story question.

The audit question that finds champions

Ask this instead: *'Tell us about a time you used AI to make your work easier, faster, or better.'*

Power users write paragraphs.

Everyone else writes a sentence.

We're not rewarding verbosity here. The point is that detail reveals lived experience. People who have built workflows have stories. They remember what they tried. They remember what broke. They have opinions.

That's your signal.

Other ways to spot champions are quieter. Listen for phrases like:

'I've been experimenting...'

'I ran it through a model...'

'I built myself a system for that...'

'I found the answer using AI...'

Those are breadcrumbs. And if you praise someone and they respond with self-deprecation (*'Oh, it's nothing, I just geeked out'*), pay attention. Humility is often camouflage for a high-value skill set. Finally, ask managers a specific question: *'Who is consistently turning things around faster, cleaner, or with fewer errors than before?'*

Speed isn't the only clue but it's often the first visible one.

And if you have adoption data across your platforms and tools, you can find clues inside usage patterns. Who's logging in regularly? Who's using the advanced features? Who's building templates and workflows? Usually it's a small cluster. That's your starting point.

Don't fall into the loudest voice trap

Here's where leadership bias quietly shapes the future. The most visible 'AI people' are often the ones who like being visible. That doesn't mean they're your best champions.

Your best champions might be introverts quietly building brilliant systems. They might be women or people of colour who don't feel safe bragging. They might be in roles that don't traditionally get platformed.

And they might not be in IT.

In fact, the champions with the most practical impact are often closest to the actual work - customer success, sales, ops, admin, project management. The people who care about getting the job done will make the tech behave.

So dig deeper than the usual suspects.

Because if you only elevate the loudest voices, you reproduce inequity at the exact moment the tool is amplifying advantage.

The 10pm experimenters

I want to go back to Heather Cannings because she clocked it on the 10pm experiments from women. Heather leads StrikeUP Canada, a free digital conference for women entrepreneurs through Nventure, a not-for-profit that supports entrepreneurs with funding and strategy. Thousands of women join the event from across Canada every year. She has data. She has stories. And she has a perspective.

When I asked her what AI adoption looks like for the women she serves, she said: *'They're using it at 10pm, 11pm. They've finished up their work day, put their kids to bed, and they're trying to get their newsletters out, their social content. They're interested and they're experimenting. But it's happening in these stolen moments. Not in a relaxed, strategic way.'*

Stolen moments.

Not a dedicated learning hour. Not a company-sponsored workshop. Not a Thursday afternoon with a latte and a tutorial.

10pm. Kids asleep. Exhausted. Still pushing one more thing across the finish line.

Heather told me: *'I don't think they have the same true access as some others because they don't have the benefit of time during the day to sit down and be really strategic about the way they're going to use it and put in that upfront time it takes to get set up and to really learn it.'*

So when we look at who's adopting AI and who isn't, we need to be honest about what we're actually measuring. Are we measuring who had the luxury of learning during work hours? Or are we measuring who's resourceful enough to figure it out at 10pm while running on fumes?

Because those 10pm experimenters? They're champions too. They're just invisible because the system wasn't designed to see them.

The imposter trap

There's another layer here that Heather Cannings named, and I want to be specific about it because it affects who comes forward. She told me: *'Women put pressure on themselves to make sure they're producing. There's this notion of imposter syndrome. "Am I an imposter if I'm using AI? If it's not my work, does it truly demonstrate the benefit I have for this organization?"'*

Read that again.

People are still worried that using AI is *cheating*.

Not worried that AI will replace them. Worried that using it well means their work doesn't count.

Heather continued: *'I think probably more so from women than from men. There's additional pressure on being judged if they're not going to do it correctly.'*

And here's what's WILD about this. When I asked Heather what women entrepreneurs (and employees with entrepreneurial side hustles) are actually doing with AI, the use cases were deeply practical. Writing better copy. Content planning. Summarizing large documents. Grants and pitches. These are business-critical tasks! But they're doing them while navigating a set of pressures that their peers in other demographics might not face. As Heather put it: '*They're looking for practical uses that they feel they're not going to get in trouble for.*' (With clients, with their peers in their day jobs, with their audiences who don't hesitate to call out AI use as a character flaw.)

Think about that in the context of champions.

If someone is afraid they'll get in trouble for using AI, they will NEVER self-identify as an AI champion. Even if they're the best one you have.

Shona Boyd (whom you met in Chapter 8) said something related that connects dots here. She told me: '*The things that make you really good at AI are those underlying skills. Reasoning. Problem solving. Question asking. Empathy. Putting yourself in someone's shoes.*'

Those are not traditionally the skills we celebrate in 'tech champions'. But they're exactly the skills that produce the best AI work. So if your champion selection process rewards confidence over competence, rewards volume over quality, rewards visibility over impact, you will miss the people who are doing the best work. And you will build an inequity into your AI future that mirrors every other inequity you've been trying to fix.

The Three R's of champion support

Okay. You've found your champions. Or at least you've started looking in the right places.

Now what?

Here's the simplest structure I know that prevents burnout and creates compounding value.

Recognition. Resourcing. Repositories.
An alliteration with heavy implications.

Recognition: name the role

Recognition is orientation. Name what they're doing as valuable. Give it a title that fits your culture: AI Champion, AI Guide, AI Pathfinder, whatever language feels human in your environment. *(If you're the kind of org that calls them 'Innovation Jedis', I won't judge. Much.)*

Then make the message explicit - this is not extra work disguised as praise. This is a meaningful contribution to the future of the company. Recognition can include inviting champions into strategy conversations. Asking for their input on governance and training. Publicly acknowledging wins.

That public part matters more than you think. Public recognition sends a signal beyond the individual. It tells the whole organization that curiosity is welcome here. Experimentation is valued. You are not going to get fired for trying something new.

In a moment where people literally fear that learning AI means training their own replacement, that signal will go a long way.

Resourcing: give time and support

This is the part most organizations skip. And then they act confused when champions disappear. If someone is spending 10 to 20 percent of their week experimenting, documenting, and helping peers, that time has to come from somewhere.

It should not come from their nights.

It should not come from their weekends.

It should not come from 'just pushing harder'.

(It should DEFINITELY not come from 10pm after the kids are in bed.)

Resourcing means adjusting goals. Updating KPIs. Sometimes updating job descriptions. Sometimes offering a budget for better tools, training, or memberships that help them do the work well.

Money is an honest signal.

Time is an even more honest one.

Remember Gazzy Amin from Chapter 10? She told her executive assistant: *'I want you to spend two hours a week learning how we can use AI to advance and scale the company.'* Not 'your job is in danger.' Not 'figure this out or else.' Two hours a week. Dedicated. Protected.

That's what resourcing looks like when a leader actually means it.

Repositories: turn personal hacks into shared assets

Repositories are where experimentation becomes organizational capability. A personal workflow that stays in one person's head is less system and more a private advantage that walks out the door when they do.

(If you did the visibility exercise from Chapter 10, the registry, you've already started this.)

Repositories are how you capture and spread learning:

Short Loom recordings that show what a workflow actually looks like in practice.

Internal 'show and tell' sessions or rituals where champions demo what they've built. *(Keep these informal. The second they feel like mandatory training, people stop coming.)*

Playbooks that document repeatable workflows in plain language.

Templates and prompt recipes stored where the whole team can find them.

A simple internal hub that answers one question: *'What do we use AI for, and how?'*

Champions should be guides, not gatekeepers

There is another trap worth naming, because I've watched it happen in real time. Sometimes leaders formalize champions and accidentally turn them into the Police! They become the people who police tool use, scold experimentation, and shut colleagues down before they've even finished their sentence. That is how you kill adoption while telling yourself you're building governance.

Shona Boyd was clear about this distinction. She said organizations need rules at every level, yes. But she also said leaders need to keep an empathetic framework around how people are feeling. Because if people think they'll be punished for experimenting, they'll just do it behind your back.

Champions should feel like guides. They should be the people others run to saying: *'Look what I built. How do I make it better?'* Not: *'Am I allowed to do this?'* Let governance live where it belongs - legal, risk, security, finance. Invite champions into those conversations. Give them a direct line to the people who can say yes to experiments. But don't load them with enforcement.

Keep champions close to the work and the people. That's where they shine.

The Champion Blueprint

Here's a practical sequence that works whether you're a ten-person team or a mid-market organization.

Step 1: Identify.
Use surveys and interviews. Ask managers. Ask peers. Look at usage patterns if you have them. Look beyond the usual suspects. Use multiple methods: surveys, nominations, self-nominations. Ask managers to think broadly, not just about who's obviously helping, but about who's quietly tinkering and who might be under the radar.

Step 2: Invite.
Reach out personally. Tell them what you've seen. Ask if they're interested. Make it an opportunity, not an obligation. People must be able to say no without consequences. Some of your best candidates will need to be convinced that this is safe.

Step 3: Define.
Clarify responsibilities and boundaries. What are they here to do? And equally important: what are they NOT responsible for? They're not the AI police. They're not full-time trainers. They're not expected to have all the answers. Spell that out.

Step 4: Resource.
Allocate 10 to 20 percent of their time. Adjust KPIs. Provide tools, training, and support. If the reward for curiosity is more work on top of an already full plate, that buys you resentment.

Step 5: Amplify.
Create visibility, repositories, and ritual mechanisms so their learning becomes shared assets. Integrate their insights into training and governance. Let them become visible symbols of what's possible.

Notice what is missing from this list: 'assign them a pilot project'. Because 'pilot' often becomes corporate code for 'do your day job plus this massive new thing for free'.

Don't do that.

Connected champions beat lonely champions

A champion alone is weak. A champion connected to legal, IT, and leadership is powerful. Connection gives them a direct line to the people who can say yes to experiments. It also protects them. They're not stuck arguing with compliance in the hallway. They can sanity check quickly and keep momentum without creating risk.

Connection also gives you something leaders rarely get in the AI era - a front-row seat to how AI is ACTUALLY being used. Not how you hope it's being used. That visibility is priceless. *(It's also the kind of intelligence that makes your next budget conversation a LOT easier.)*

And connection means something else too. It means champions aren't isolated from each other. If you have more than one *(and you should)*, connect them. Let them share notes, compare failures, and celebrate small wins.

The moment someone realizes they're not the only one figuring this out, everything changes. The fear drops. The pace picks up. The learning compounds.

What the support system should actually look like

I asked Heather Cannings what kinds of support systems would actually help the women she works with. Her answer was practical and a little uncomfortable for anyone who designs training programs.

She said: '*You need to take out the assumption that there is unlimited time. That people have access to teams. That they have great internet. You need to start looking at how they can utilize and work from real constraints.*'

She told me about the data from StrikeUP's digital conference. Some attendees join from mobile. They're in their car. They're eating lunch in a back room. They're in a storage room of their business. And when she described what women entrepreneurs actually want from AI support, it wasn't cutting-edge agentic frameworks, it was practical, immediate use cases connected to the work they're already doing.

This is what champion support should look like for EVERYONE. Meet people where they are. Start with what they actually do. Remove the assumption that everyone has the same starting conditions.

Heather said something near the end of our conversation that I think belongs in every leadership playbook: *'I would like to see AI be a quiet force in the background for women so that they can actually have more control over their time and their income.'*

Your move: the one conversation

Do this THIS week. Think of one person in your world who fits the suspiciously quick description. Invite them for a short chat. Coffee. A walk. A fifteen-minute call. Whatever works. Ask: *'What have you been trying with AI lately?'* Then ask: *'How can we make space for you to keep experimenting like this, and help others learn from it?'* That second question is the fulcrum. Helen Patterson would call it a mentor moment. One conversation that changes the trajectory.

And here's the thing. When you have that conversation, pay attention to who you're NOT having it with. Ask yourself: who else in my organization might be doing this work, quietly, at 10pm, without anyone noticing?

Go find them too.

One conversation is enough to start your champion programme.

Even if you never call it that.

CHAPTER 12

Does AI make you more or less creative?

Why the creative advantage isn't "more content". It's better judgement.

I'm going to tell you something that might sting a little. That blog post you published last Tuesday? The one AI wrote in four minutes flat? The one you barely glanced at before hitting publish because you were running late and it sounded fine?

People could tell.

Not because they ran it through a detector.

Not because some watermark gave you away.

Not the em dash or the sentence structures either!

But because it had no SPINE.

No opinion.

No rough edges.

No you.

It read like a thousand other posts that week. And the internet did what the internet does with things that blend in.

It scrolled right past.

Here's the thing, folx. People keep asking me the same question, dressed up in different outfits. Does AI make you more creative? Or does it make you bland?

I've heard both takes. LOUDLY. And I understand why the debate won't die. Because both are true.

AI can make you wildly more creative. It can also make you frighteningly average.

The difference is not the model. It's not the subscription tier. It's not some magical prompt template someone's selling for $47 on X.

It's the driver.

If you use AI to replace thinking, you get generic trash. If you use it to expand thinking, you get something close to a superpower.

That is the core of this chapter. And it's also the bridge between creativity and ROI. Because in founder-led teams and small-to-mid organizations, the real return on AI is not more output, it's better outcomes. Better decisions. Better positioning. Better clarity. Better work that people actually WANT.

And those outcomes come from a very human skill.

Taste.

Paintbrush vs. Photocopier

Here is a question I use for diagnosing your AI use. *Are you using AI as a paintbrush, or as a photocopier?*

A photocopier duplicates what already exists. Fast. Clean. Predictable. Average.

A paintbrush explores. It mixes. It experiments. It makes something that didn't exist five minutes ago. It requires a hand.

If you treat AI like a photocopier, you will scale mediocrity. You will get efficient at being boring. And you'll become easier to ignore. Because the internet does not reward the 10,000th version of a safe idea. It rewards point of view.

If you treat AI like a paintbrush, you shorten the distance between blank page and brave draft. You give yourself more angles than your tired brain could produce alone.

Then you choose.

That choosing is where creativity lives now. In curation.

My friend Suzanne Huber, who is a go-to-market consultant and a writer of 15+ years, said '*That's where you need that craftsmanship to come in and use it and not take that first draft*.' I know that a lot of the reason AI-assisted content gets such a bad rap is because often the error of considering a first draft from AI as good enough is made because of content factory level thinking, where no real subject matter expertise lives and where people are just churning out a bunch of stuff.

And here's the kicker that Suzanne calls out. '*The problem is that when it's generating all of this content, it LOOKS really credible. It sounds great. And conceptually, unless you know the topic, it could be great. But it could be entirely fluff.*'

That's the photocopier in action. Looks sharp. Sounds smart. Says absolutely nothing.

AI Creates Options. Humans Create Meaning.

AI does not create creativity. It creates options. Options are not the same as insight. They're raw material. They're the starting point.

Humans provide the taste, judgement, and discernment to choose the right option. Humans decide what matters. Humans decide what to reject.

In the AI era, the creative act is often not 'make something from nothing'. It's 'spot the gem in a pile of rocks'. Then polish it until it's unmistakably yours.

That is taste.

Taste is what you emphasize. Taste is what you refuse. Taste is what you keep weird on purpose.

(That last one is my favourite. The deliberate weirdness. The thing that makes your brand YOUR brand and not a template with a logo swap.)

Taste is also what protects your brand from drifting into that generic, corporate, oddly cheerful voice that makes people say, 'I can tell AI wrote this'.

When people say that, they don't mean they detected a robot. They mean they couldn't detect a human.

Creativity is how organizations stay distinct.

Creativity is vastly underrated. Leaders sometimes treat it like a nice-to-have. Like it belongs in the same category as ping pong tables and motivational posters. But creativity is how organizations stay distinct when tools become commoditized. When your competitors have access to the same models, the same features, and the same sparkle icons, your advantage cannot be "we use AI". Everybody uses AI. That's like saying your advantage is "we use email".

Your advantage becomes how you think, how you decide, how you communicate, and how you hold a point of view under pressure.

That's the ROI.

(More on that in the next chapter.)

The Driver's Wheel

If you want a simple mental model that holds up under stress, use this one. I call it The Driver's Wheel and it has four parts.

Input. What raw material are you feeding the machine? Your notes. Your experience. Your point of view. Your constraints. The quality of what goes IN determines the quality of what comes OUT. *(Garbage in... say it with me... garbage out!)*

Intent. What are you actually trying to do? And I don't mean "create content". That's too vague. I mean things like: Shift perception. Earn trust. Simplify a decision. Sell with integrity. The clearer your intent, the sharper the output.

Iteration. Do you do one prompt and ship? Or do you challenge, refine, and push? The people getting great results are not doing one-and-done. They're going back. They're saying "make this punchier" or "argue the opposite" or "that's too generic, try again".

Inspection. Do you edit like a human? Do you check tone, truth, and usefulness? Do you read it out loud and ask yourself "does this sound like me?" *(If you've never tried reading your AI output out loud, try it today. You will immediately hear the parts that don't sound like you. They'll stick out like a sore thumb.)*

When creativity dies in AI workflows, it's usually because one of these four things broke. The input was thin. The intent was vague. Iteration never happened. Inspection was skipped.

The driver stepped out of the car.

What to Do: Five Ways to Use AI Like a Paintbrush

1. Use it as a sparring partner.

Stop asking for validation. *(AI's going to say yes to what you said. It always says yes. AI is a chronic people-pleaser.)* Instead, ask it to argue the opposite. Ask it to find the holes in your logic. Ask it what you're not seeing. A sparring partner is not there to compliment you. It's there to sharpen you.

This is one of the highest-ROI uses of AI for leaders because it improves JUDGEMENT, not just output.

2. Turn it into a possibility engine.
When you feel stuck, don't ask for the answer. Ask for range. Ask for 20 angles. Ask for metaphors. Ask for surprising structures. Ask for unconventional openings. Ask for the version that would annoy your industry.

You're widening your aperture. You're giving your brain more clay to shape.

3. Generate constraints on purpose.
Creativity LOVES constraints. Freedom is overrated when you're staring at a blank page. *(Trust me. I've stared at many blank pages. The blank page always wins when you have infinite freedom.)* Ask for constraints like: "Give me three eight-word active voice sentences. No commas." Constraints force precision. Precision creates voice. I do this ALL the time, by the way. The amount of sh!t that gets trimmed away when you impose a word count is genuinely magical.

4. Use it as a remix assistant.
This is where AI is genuinely delightful. Feed it your raw thoughts and ask it to remix: *"Turn this into a framework." "Turn this into a debate." "Turn this into a checklist." "Turn this into a short story." "Turn this into a training exercise."*

AI handles format. You focus on the insight.

5. Treat the first draft as raw material.
The first output is rarely the work. The work starts after generation. This is where SO many teams lose the plot. They ship the first draft unchanged. They call it efficiency. It's not. It's abandonment.

If you want AI to make you more creative, you must stay in the loop long enough to shape the thing into something you'd actually stand behind. Something you'd put your NAME on.

AI Doesn't Do Courage

Creativity requires two things. Taste. And courage. AI has neither.

It can give you raw material. It can suggest bolder ideas than you would dare to say out loud on a tired Thursday. But it cannot choose the brave path for you. It cannot take the reputational risk. It cannot decide to be specific when generic would be safer.

If your work feels bland, don't blame the machine.

Look at where you outsourced courage.

Did you sand off the sharp edges? Did you remove your actual opinion? Did you avoid naming the real tension because it felt impolite? AI will happily help you write around your own fear. It's VERY good at that. It'll give you the safe version, the diplomatic version, the version that says nothing while appearing to say something.

And people are getting terrible advice that compounds this problem. Marketer and entrepreneurs Gary Vaynerchuk is out there telling people that now that AI can produce content at scale, you should be writing 50 posts a day to test things. Just because you can doesn't mean you should, folx.

So you have to drive. You have to be the one who decides what's worth saying, what angle matters, what risk is worth taking. YOU are your courage. AI just makes it faster to get the words out once you've decided to be brave.

The Mirror

AI is holding up a mirror.

If the output is boring, it's often because the input was boring. Not because YOU are boring. Because you were cautious. Because you were vague. Because you fed it thin material and hoped it would somehow create depth.

The good news? This is totally fixable.

If you're feeling stuck creatively, don't quit AI. Don't throw up your hands and say "this thing is useless".

Change the prompt.

Tell it to make it stranger. Tell it to make it truer. Tell it to make it more YOU.

And if you're really feeling bold, tell it to make it the version that scares you a little bit.

The creativity is not inside the machine. It never was.

It's in the hands of the driver.

So put your hands on the wheel, folx. And drive like you mean it.

CHAPTER 13

ROI Beyond Time Saved

The metrics that survive CFO scrutiny.

We touched on this briefly... You know that beautiful slide in your AI update deck? The one that says "We saved 200 hours last quarter" in big, bold font with a little upward-trending arrow next to it?

Your CFO does not care.

Okay. That's not entirely fair. Your CFO cares a LITTLE. In the same way they care about the office recycling program. It's nice. It's a decent thing. But it is not what they came to the meeting to hear.

What they came to hear is: what changed in the business?

And "we saved 200 hours" does not answer that question. It answers a DIFFERENT question, which is: "did we get faster at doing stuff?" And faster at doing stuff is not the same as doing BETTER stuff. Or doing the RIGHT stuff. Or doing stuff that moves the needle in any direction that matters.

Here's the deal, folx. Time saved is table stakes. It's the easiest number to collect. It's the most intuitive metric in the world. Everybody gets it.

"We used to spend five hours on this and now we spend two." Cool. But it doesn't tell anybody WHERE those three hours went. And if nobody redirected those three hours into something that actually matters, you didn't save time.

You just freed it up so it could get eaten by Slack messages and unnecessary meetings.

Time saved, a lot like money saved, won't compound unless you invest it.

Why "Hours Saved" Keeps Failing You

There are three specific reasons why time saved falls flat in the boardroom. And once you see them, you can't unsee them.

Reason One: Saved time doesn't automatically convert to value. A time-saving metric is a capacity metric. Not a value metric. Value only shows up when you DELIBERATELY reinvest that capacity into something that changes outcomes. Things like customer experience. Speed to market. Better decisions. Higher quality. Reduced risk. MORE REST!

If nobody can point to where those 200 hours went, then "200 hours saved" is just a number that sounds impressive and changes nothing.

Kirsten Schmidtke, sales leadership consultant, talked to me about how AI should help us *"shift from the thinking of output to outcomes."* Because if we're focused on output, we're just measuring productivity for productivity's sake. *"A really effective leader who's generating outcomes and creating change and impact,"* Kirsten said, *"they're probably not doing things for the sake of doing things."*

That's the whole problem with measuring hours saved in isolation. It counts the DOING without ever asking what the doing was FOR.

Reason Two: It creates the Busy Work Trap.
Kirsten also made a connection that I think is brilliant and honestly a little uncomfortable. She compared the AI time-saving trap to what happened during COVID. *"If we were at home at our desks on our laptop every day, then why couldn't we pack every hour with a meeting?"* she said. *"And so I can see that it's similar. If we have access to something that's going to save us time, then we better fill it. We better fill whatever we've saved."*

(Can we have a moment of silence for all the Zoom meetings that should have been emails that should have been Slack messages that should have been nothing at all?)

When teams save time without a reinvestment plan, they fill the gap with more busy work. Faster busy work is still busy work, folx.

AI doesn't automatically create strategy.

It creates ROOM for strategy.

Room is not the same as results.

Reason Three: It punishes high performers.
This one is the sneakiest. The first people to save time are usually the people who adopt early, experiment bravely, and systematize like their lives depend on it. The Divers, if you're thinking back to our archetypes from Chapter 1.

And what happens when they visibly become faster? Come on. You know the answer. They get rewarded with MORE WORK. Which teaches the entire organization a very dangerous lesson - hide your efficiency. Keep your head down. Don't let anyone see how fast you can do things because all it gets you is more things.

If your only metric for AI success is speed, you accidentally build a culture where the smart move is to LOOK busy rather than BE efficient. And then your champions burn out. And your flywheel stalls. And everyone says, *"See? AI didn't work."*

Build the Stack, Not the Slide

You need more than one number because AI changes multiple variables at once. It affects quality. Risk. Speed. Decisions. Learning. A single metric can't carry that complexity. Here's the ROI stack instead. Five metrics, designed to translate cleanly into executive language without losing truth.

Metric 1: Quality Lift

Definition: Improvement in output quality at the same headcount.

Quality can sound subjective until you measure it using operational proxies. And operational proxies are just a fancy way of saying "the sh!t you can actually count". Track your revision cycles. How many rounds from draft to approval? If you used to go through four rounds and now you go through two, that's a quality lift. You also created capacity. And you did it without hiring.

Track your error rate. Typos, factual errors, broken links, incorrect fields, compliance mistakes. As a content agency, one tiny example I can give you is proofreading. We used to spend SO much time on this.

In under three years, with tools like Copilot and Gemini built into the stuff we already use, I feel like it's been a REALLY long time since I've come across a typo in our work. We've basically eradicated something that used to be a whole job.

Track rework time. Hours spent fixing preventable issues. If that number is shrinking, quality is going up.

Track customer or stakeholder satisfaction. NPS scores. CSAT. Internal quality scores. Whatever your organization already uses to assess *"was this good?"*

Your CFO translation: Higher quality output with the exact same headcount. That's capacity expansion, not a one-off productivity hack.

Metric 2: Risk Reduction

AI gets a LOT of grief for introducing risk. And it does. *(We talked about this in the governance chapters. Shadow AI is real. People are pasting sensitive data into personal ChatGPT instances and we all need to stop pretending that's not happening.)*

But AI also REDUCES risk. And that's worth measuring.

Track near misses. Issues you caught before they became incidents. This is the invisible metric, and it's one of the most powerful ones you have. Because near misses quantify the mistake that didn't ship. The contract clause that got flagged before signing. The compliance issue that got caught at draft stage instead of after it went to the client.

Track compliance exceptions. Policy breaches, missing disclosures, incorrect claims.

Track security incidents tied to data handling. And track legal load. Escalations. Contract issues. Time spent by your legal team correcting avoidable problems.

Jennifer Hufnagel, the AI educator and has trained over 4,000 people whom you met in chapter 5, told me something that stuck. She said when she talks to companies about their AI adoption, she breaks it into three stages: AI awareness, AI readiness, and AI adoption. And the readiness stage is where a LOT of the risk mapping happens. *"What is your existing software stack? Where is your data? How dirty is your data?"* she said. That due diligence is RISK hygiene. And it's measurable. It's about both AI for Efficiency and AI for Opportunity.

Your CFO translation: Fewer costly failures. Fewer expensive mistakes. Fewer escalations to legal. Risk reduction behaves like an insurance policy that pays for itself.

Metric 3: Speed to Opportunity

This is NOT the same as hours saved. This is how quickly you can turn intent into revenue-relevant action. Track the time from idea to first draft to customer touch. How long does it take to respond to an RFP? How long does it take to launch a campaign? How long does a sales cycle run from lead to close?

If your team can respond to an RFP in 24 hours instead of five days, you changed your competitive POSITION. Revenue comes to the door sooner. The CFO sees that immediately.

Kirsten Schmidtke had a great way of framing this from the sales side. She talked about how AI can shorten contracts, debriefs, and executive summaries. *"Things that are just going to allow us to move the sales cycle faster,"* she said. The goal isn't to remove humans from the process. It's to *"take more of the thinking out of it so that they can be more present to supporting and helping the customer."*

That's the flip. Speed to opportunity is about removing the friction that sits between your intent and your customer's experience. I lived this myself, by the way. In 2025, I rebranded my company. The last time I did a rebrand, maybe seven years ago, it took MONTHS. Months of thinking. Months of work. Months of implementation. This time around? Days. A few intense days. Because we had clear direction and AI handled the grunt work while we focused on the strategy.

That is speed to opportunity in real life.

Your CFO translation: Revenue hits the bank sooner. Speed reduces sales cycle drag. That's real money.

Metric 4: Decision Velocity

This is the stealth ROI category. And it is HUGELY underrated. Organizations leak value through indecision. Every day something sits "in progress" without moving is a day of drag on your entire system. And nobody puts "we couldn't make up our minds for three weeks" on a budget sheet. But the cost is real.

Track time-to-decision in recurring meetings. How many decisions actually get made per meeting versus how many get punted to "let's circle back"?

Track stuck work. Open your project management tool. Look at how long tasks sit in "In Progress" without changing status. If something's been there for two weeks and nobody's touched it, that's a ghost.

Track aging reports. Track confidence levels. A confident team executes. A hesitant team stalls. Stall is measurable. AI helps here because it improves clarity. It can summarize inputs, compare options, model scenarios, and highlight trade-offs. When people see their choices clearly, they decide faster.

Your CFO translation: Less drag. Fewer delays. More projects moving without escalation.

Metric 5: Learning Velocity

This is the compounding metric. And honestly, if I had to pick just ONE metric from this stack to show leadership, it might be this one.

Because learning velocity tells you whether your AI adoption is an event or a capability.

Track your adoption curve. How fast are people moving from "aware" to "competent"? Jennifer Hufnagel told me that despite some surveys claiming 80 or 90% AI adoption in Canada, "*At the end of the day, I'm not sure who they're talking to because they're not in the rooms that I'm in.*" (And she, my friends, is in a LOT of rooms talking about AI.) When she asks people whether they've used a reasoning model, have a paid version of a Generative AI tool, or if they've created automations, the answers are *"still very, very low"*.

So the gap between HAVING tools and USING tools effectively is massive. And learning velocity measures how fast you're closing that gap.

Track workflow production. How many documented AI workflows does your organization create per month?

Track workflow diffusion. This is the big one. How many of those workflows are used by more than 10 people? Because if one person on your marketing team has a brilliant content workflow and nobody else knows about it, that's a hero story. It's nice. But it doesn't compound. If 25 people across three departments are using a version of that workflow, THAT'S organizational learning. That's the flywheel.

Track time to production. How long does it take from a new capability being introduced to it showing up in REAL work?

Your CFO translation: This has gone beyond one-off experimentation into capability being built and spreading. Hero stories are cute. Infrastructure gets funded.

Building the Dashboard: Three Layers

A dashboard is only useful if it tells a coherent story. Not every number belongs on the main page. *(And for the love of everything, please don't put 47 metrics on one slide and call it a "dashboard". That's a crime scene.)*

Use three layers.

Layer One: Leading Indicators. These tell you if the system is taking root.

Workflow usage. Adoption rate. Learning velocity. These are your behavioural and adoption metrics. They're the early signals.

Layer Two: Operational Indicators. These tell you if the process is actually performing.

Cycle time. Revision counts. Error rate. Stuck work duration. These are the nuts and bolts.

Layer Three: Business Outcomes. These tell you if it's worth funding.

Pipeline influence. Time to market. Cost of service. Margin impact. Risk events avoided or reduced.

You need all three layers. Leading indicators without business outcomes is just vibes. Business outcomes without leading indicators is just luck you can't replicate. When your dashboard tells this three-layered story, AI stops being a cost conversation and becomes an investment conversation.

The Invisible ROI: First-Order vs. Second-Order Benefits

Time saved is usually first-order ROI. It's visible. It's immediate. It's easy to describe. Somebody used AI and it took less time. Done.

The REAL ROI is often second-order. And second-order benefits are sneaky because they're harder to see. But they're where the money is.

We talked a little about the mistake that didn't ship.

The contract clause that got flagged before signing.

The decision made today instead of next week.

The faster response that won the deal.

The reduction in rework that quietly freed capacity nobody even noticed.

Gazzy Amin, entrepreneur and GTM strategist, talked about this from a small business angle. She walked her AI through her ENTIRE sales process. Every call. Every email. Every payment. And then she asked it, "What are some ways I could be automating? Which parts of this should I automate to make it a better client experience?"

"I could have never thought of this on my own," she said. *"I would have had to pay multiple people, but AI was able to do that very quickly."*

That's second-order ROI. She uncovered a system she didn't know she was missing. And that system now compounds every single day. Gazzy also dropped this absolute gem for small business owners: *"If everything is in your head, you're in trouble. Because if you have a headache one day, the whole business is f^cked."*

(I mean. She's not wrong.)

If you only count first-order ROI, you will underfund the work that creates compounding advantage. And you'll keep telling the same "we saved some hours" story while your competitors are quietly building systems that multiply value.

Measuring "Stuck Work" (A Simple Method)

This is a fast, practical exercise that most teams can do THIS WEEK. Open your project management tool. Pick a workstream with a lot of "In Progress" items. Measure how long tasks sit without changing status.

Then introduce a lightweight AI unblocker. Something like: summarize what's done, identify missing inputs, draft next-step options, surface the decision required, propose a short plan.

If the average "In Progress" duration drops, you just increased decision velocity.

That is ROI most teams never count.

And it takes about ten minutes to set up.

This, and all the other mini exercises in this book are in one easy place for you to access. Scan the QR code below or visit: https://wearenorthlightai.com/swan-dive-backwards

CHAPTER 14

The AI Gender Gap Nobody's Closing Fast Enough

It's 11pm.

The dishes are done. The kids are in bed. The day job is logged off. The mental load of being everything to everyone has been temporarily shelved. *(Temporarily. It'll be back at 6am.)*

And now, finally, in this stolen sliver of quiet, she opens her laptop and tries to learn AI.

Not in a relaxed, strategic way. Not in a well-resourced corporate training room with coffee and a facilitator and a two-hour block on the calendar which is mandatory. She's doing it on the couch, half-exhausted, with one eye on the hallway in case someone needs water or has a nightmare.

This is what AI adoption looks like for millions of women. Women entrepreneurs, side giggers, gig economy workers.

Stolen moments. Not strategy sessions.

I need you to sit with that for a second before we go any further.

The 25% Gap

Here's the stat. Women are adopting AI at approximately 25% lower rates than men as of the end of 2025. And when you first read that, it's tempting to think, *"Well, women need to get on it."* It's tempting to frame this as a motivation problem. A curiosity deficit. A *"they just need to try harder"* situation.

It is NONE of those things.

When I sat down with Heather Cannings, whom you've met earlier in the book, the Women's Entrepreneurship Program Lead at Nventure and the force behind StrikeUP (a free digital conference for women entrepreneurs that draws thousands from across Canada and beyond), she gave me data that reframed everything.

The women ARE showing up. They ARE curious. They ARE putting in the work. They're just doing it while exhausted, at the end of a day where they've already been a caregiver, an employee, a manager, a partner, a household operator, and seventeen other things.

"Women are resilient," Heather said. *"They'll find a way."* And I believe her. But resilient should not be a synonym for "expected to do everything, including learning new technology, on zero bandwidth".

It's Systemic. Not Personal.

When I say the 25% gap is another version of the wage gap, some folx push back on that. So let me be specific. The gap is about capability.

It's about time. Access. Psychological safety. And systems that were not designed with women's actual lives in mind.

Heather Cannings broke this down in layers. First: women are juggling multiple roles. Multiple jobs. Caregiving. All of that. And they're still expected to be upskilling in their spare time.

(What spare time? Seriously. Point to it on the calendar. I'll wait.)

Second: there's the confidence piece. And this one cuts deep. Women are more likely to feel like AI is cheating. Imposter syndrome meets AI. And the result is that women are learning AI later and they're learning it while simultaneously wondering whether they're allowed to use it. Whether it counts. Whether someone will judge them for it.

Chris McMartin, the National Lead for Scotiabank's Women Initiative for Business Banking, was even more blunt about this when she joined me on the podcast. And I love Chris because she does NOT sugarcoat. *"I think one of our biggest downfalls, in my personal opinion, is that we're afraid to ask the questions,"* she said. *"We're afraid for anyone to know we don't know the answer. We're afraid that people will think, well, why doesn't she know that? We're afraid to look silly."*

And so what happens? Women use AI at about 1% of its capability. They write Instagram posts with it. Maybe a newsletter. Because THAT much they can do without asking anyone for help. But locking in? Using it to change their strategy, their finances, their growth trajectory? *"I don't think so,"* Chris said. *"Because we don't want to ask anybody."*

And here's where I need to make something very clear, because when we quote stats like "25% lower adoption" it can sound like we're blaming the victim. We are NOT. This is a SYSTEMS problem wearing a personal problem disguise.

The Job Displacement Danger Nobody Wants to Name

Okay, let me get into the part that really keeps me up at night. *(Side note: for over 5 years, I hosted a podcast called 'The 4am Report' where we asked marketers and founders 'what keeps you up at night'. And I rarely ever answered that question myself.)* When people talk about jobs that AI might displace, they throw around categories like admin roles, research assistants, entry-level communications, data entry, and social media management.

Look at those categories. Now think about who is disproportionately represented in those roles.

Women. When we juxtapose that with the fact that women are already adopting AI at lower rates, you start to see a very dangerous picture forming. The people most at risk of displacement are also the people with the least time, access, and psychological safety to upskill.

If we're not careful, AI widens the gap. It strips away more of the power and equity that wasn't even fully established in the first round.

"It's a difficult balance", Heather told me, *"because AI creates incredible opportunities, but it really does put pressure on those roles that are primarily represented by women. Administrative roles, creative roles. That can be very scary for people when that's their livelihood."*

So. What do we do about it?

The Flip: Why This Moment Is Also MASSIVE Opportunity

I refuse to let this chapter live in doom. Because the opportunity here is actually enormous if we're willing to see it. And if we're willing to build the support systems that make it real.

First: the barriers to entry have never been lower. You don't need a computer science degree. You don't need to code. You don't need a $50,000 training budget. You need a laptop and curiosity and someone who will meet you where you're at. That's it. That is literally it. AI has democratized access to tools that used to cost tens of thousands of dollars. Grant writing. Market research. Content strategy. Business planning. Financial analysis. All of it is now accessible to anyone with an internet connection and the willingness to learn.

Gazzy Amin, founder of Sales Beyond Scripts, put it beautifully when we talked. *"What a beautiful time to be a woman,"* she said. Gazzy talked about how AI opened doors for her as a young woman of colour building an online business. *"It's people like you and I that are committed to sharing this"*, she told me, *"creating events for women to talk about AI - masterclasses, masterminds - to make sure that women are at the forefront."*

And she's right. The shift after the pandemic already opened huge doors for women, especially moms, to build something different. AI supercharges that.

Second: there is actual MONEY available to fund this.

Chris McMartin made a point on the podcast that I think a lot of women entrepreneurs need to hear, and I want to say it loudly for the folx in the back. *"The grants out there that are available for making technology advancements in your businesses are huge",* she said. *"Start there. And also any sort of hiring too. That's all covered in grants a lot of the time."*

And then she said the thing that I think is the real barrier: *"The opportunity for grants is something that our women entrepreneurs often don't think about. They say, 'Oh, that's not for me. I'm not a tech company.'"* Chris's response? *"Grants aren't only for tech companies. More grants go to tech companies, but I will also argue that more tech companies APPLY for grants."*

I'll admit I've been in the same camp. Because the process of applying for a grant used to be a massive pain in the a$$. It was hours of research, hours of preparation, hours of answering questions. The effort-to-maybe-reward ratio felt terrible.

But guess what tool can help you write a grant application in a fraction of the time?

Yeah.

AI literally solves the barrier to accessing the funding that pays for AI. If that's not a flywheel, I don't know what is.

Heather's Vision (And Why It Matters)

Heather Cannings said to me, *"The big goal for women is not just using AI, but helping shape how it's actually designed. In a way that makes sense for their reality. Built that way from the start."*

I love this because it reframes the entire conversation. It's not "women need to adopt AI faster" It's "AI needs to be designed with women's actual lives in mind", Those are two VERY different statements. And the second one puts the responsibility where it belongs - on the builders, the funders, the associations, the support systems. Not on the woman who's trying to learn a new tool at 10pm after putting three kids to bed.

Heather also said something that stuck with me: removing even five to ten hours of repeatable tasks for a small business owner can be a massive change in their lifestyle and their business. *"That's huge for women entrepreneurs that are balancing caregiving and a daytime job."*

Five to ten hours. That's the difference between barely surviving and actually having space to think strategically. And AI can deliver that. TODAY. Right now. With tools that are free or nearly free.

I for one will be slaying dragons to help as many women as possible to carve that out in their weeks.

Mini Exercise: The Permission Slip

This one is for anyone who has ever felt like using AI is somehow cheating. Or who has hesitated to raise their hand because they didn't want to look like they didn't know something.

Write yourself a permission slip. Literally. On paper. Right now.

Here's a template if you need one:

"I give myself permission to use every tool available to me. I give myself permission to ask questions, make mistakes, and learn. I give myself permission to stop apologizing for getting help. The work is still mine. The judgment is still mine. The strategy is still mine. The tool just makes me faster."

Now here's the second part.

Send it to one other woman. A colleague. A friend. A founder you admire. Your sister. Someone in your DMs. Anyone.

Because Chris McMartin is right. We need to stop shying away from what we don't think we know. And we need to start saying yes. Yes to the conversation. Yes to the learning. Yes to the asking.

And if you need somewhere to start, here's Chris's advice: *"Ask AI questions. Nobody's judging you that way."* That might be the lowest-risk, highest-reward first step any woman can take.

This, and all the other mini exercises in this book are in one easy place for you to access. Scan the QR code below or visit: https://wearenorthlightai.com/swan-dive-backwards

The Call to Organizations

If you're a leader reading this chapter and thinking "this doesn't apply to my company", I'd gently push back.

Look at your adoption data by gender. If you're not tracking that, start.

Look at your training formats. Are they accessible to people with care-giving responsibilities? People who can't block four hours on a Tuesday? People who might need to join from mobile?

Look at your champions and early adopters. Are they all the same demographic? If so, you're building a flywheel that only spins for some of your people.

And look at the roles in your organization that are most likely to be affected by AI automation. Who holds those roles? What upskilling pathways are you offering them? What FUNDED upskilling pathways?

CHAPTER 15

35,000 Reasons for Hope

While the headlines sold fear, the data told a different story.

Here is my least favourite headline format from the years since OpenAI released ChatGPT: *"AI Will Replace X Million Jobs By [Insert Year That's Close Enough To Scare You]."*

You've seen it. I've seen it. Your mom has seen it. Your uncle who barely uses email has DEFINITELY seen it, and he's been forwarding it to the family group chat with a "see? I told you so" energy that nobody asked for.

And look. I'm not going to sit here and tell you those headlines are entirely wrong. Jobs will change. Some roles will shrink. Some will disappear. That's real. I'm not going to pretend it isn't.

But here's what those headlines never, EVER include.

The other half of the story.

The Number Nobody's Talking About

Helen Patterson, senior HR leader, and one of the most deeply human-centered thinkers I've had on the podcast told me, *"I looked up AI policy and AI policy roles on Indeed, which is a recruitment platform, and it came up with around 35,000 jobs posted."*

35,000 jobs? On one platform??? For people who can write AI policy?! That is WILD! Because in the exact same news cycle where every other headline is screaming about job losses, there are TENS OF THOUSANDS of new roles being posted for skills that didn't even exist three years ago.

And it's not just AI policy writing. Helen pointed to the broader ecosystem that's spinning up around this. *"If you look at all the universities and the colleges and all the other new forms of academia, there's programs, there's courses. Within engineering, within every role, there's going to be these new AI-forward positions."*

So while the fear narrative says "your job is going away", the actual labour market is saying "we desperately need people who can do THIS new thing."

Both things are true at the same time. But only one of them makes the headlines.

The Milk Delivery Man

Chris McMartin (Business Banking National Lead, The Scotiabank Women Initiative) put this in perspective with an analogy. *"There used to be milk delivery,"* Chris told me. *"A man used to show up to everyone's door with bottles in a thing and put them and come pick up your bottles. That doesn't exist anymore. But those folks went and did other things. There's going to be new things that we need people to do. With AI, there's going to be new things that happen. New jobs. New opportunities. We need new people to train us how to use AI. There's going to be new adventures and new things to do. Maybe there's not going to be some of the jobs that there are now. But there's also no typewriter ribbon people, because we don't use typewriters anymore."*

Typewriter ribbon people.

When's the last time you thought about the person who manufactured typewriter ribbons? Or the person who delivered ice blocks to homes before refrigerators?

Those jobs vanished. And the world didn't end. New jobs showed up that nobody could have predicted. The people adapted. They always do.

Chris McMartin connected this directly to the 35,000 number that Helen Patterson surfaced. When I told her about those Indeed postings for AI policy roles, she lit up. "*That's an upskill right there*", she said. "*If you're already some type of policy writer, or if you're already someone who understands grant writing, it's like a hop. You're just upskilling. It's something a little bit different.*"

A hop. Not a canyon. Not a complete career reinvention. A hop.

"*And that goes to so many other things*", Chris continued. "*What about facilitators who facilitate training sessions? What about educators? There's going to be new opportunities that are maybe THIS much away from what you do now.*" She held her fingers close together when she said that. Like, a centimetre apart.

That's the distance between "my job is at risk" and "I have a new, better job". And most people don't know how small that gap actually is.

We Have Literally Done This Before

Let's go on a tiny history detour. Every single time humanity has had a major technological shift, the same pattern plays out. Fear. Headlines. Panic about job losses. And then... adaptation. New industries. New roles. A net increase in both jobs and quality of life.

The Industrial Revolution? People were terrified. *"We'll waste away! What will we do with our bodies if machines do the physical work?"* And here we are. Maybe a little less fit than we should be (fair), but we didn't turn into puddles of cells on the floor.

Calculators? I'm old enough to remember when the educational debate was whether students should be ALLOWED to use them. The fear was that nobody would be able to do math ever again. And now we all carry one in our pocket. On a device that is also a camera, a map, a library, a recording studio, and apparently a milk delivery replacement (hey, Instacart!).

I am also old enough to remember how, at one stage maybe a decade ago, people picked items to pack into delivery boxes inside of behemoths like Amazon. Along came robotic process automation. People lost jobs. But then new jobs were created. I often reference this in trainings and speaking engagements about how AI is robotic process automation for the creative mind! Kinda like how Iron Man talks to Jarvis. There's no actual doing of things on the computer for Tony Stark. We're getting a lot closer to that.

The "Purple Person" and the Jobs That Didn't Exist

Okay so here's where it gets really interesting. Because it's not just that existing jobs are being preserved with a little AI sprinkled on top. Entirely NEW categories of work are emerging. Roles that literally did not exist before this wave hit.

Melissa Penton is a change manager, AI readiness lead, and one of the most thoughtfully curious humans I've spoken with about this stuff. She (a Candian) works at Sun Life in Ireland, she writes a Substack called "Confessions of an AI User" (love the double entendre of that title), and she described herself in a way that I think captures an entire new career archetype. *"I am a purple person",* Melissa told me. *"That is a name for people who sit between the tech world and the business world and love to be able to communicate what's happening to both sides."*

A purple person.

I'd be very quick to identify as a purple person. I am not a tech person. But I am a knowledge translator. Now that's arguably one of the most valuable roles in any organization trying to adopt AI. Someone who speaks both languages. Who can translate between the engineers building the tools and the humans who need to actually use them. Who can sit in a room full of executives and explain what's possible, and then sit in a room full of practitioners and explain why it matters.

That's a job that AI will be creating in the millions.

And think about all the other roles that are emerging in this space. AI readiness consultants. AI literacy trainers. AI policy writers *(all 35,000 of them so far).* AI ethics advisors. AI implementation coaches. AI audit specialists. Change managers with AI expertise. HR professionals who understand how to build AI governance. Educators who can teach humans how to work alongside machines.

None of these existed in 2021.

ALL of them exist now.

And the demand is only growing.

The Real Headline: It's a Hop, Not a Cliff

I want to come back to Chris McMartin's word because I think it's the most important reframe in this chapter.

A hop.

The distance between where you are now and where these new opportunities live is not a cliff. It's not a canyon. You don't need to go back to school for four years. You don't need a computer science degree. You don't need to become a completely different person.

You need to hop.

If you're a policy writer, you can learn AI policy. If you're a facilitator, you can learn to facilitate AI training. If you're an educator, you can learn to teach AI literacy. If you're in HR, you can learn AI governance. If you're a consultant, you can add AI readiness to your toolkit.

And here's where I need to be direct with you, reader. If you're sitting in a role right now and you're worried about what AI means for your future, I need you to hear me. The worry is valid. The fear is understandable. But the response should not be to freeze. The response should be to take one tiny hop.

Because the organizations that are hiring for these 35,000 roles? They're not looking for AI experts with ten years of experience. *(Nobody has ten years of experience in GenAI in 2026.)* They're looking for smart, adaptable humans who understand their domain AND can layer AI thinking on top of it.

That's you. That's your existing expertise plus a willingness to learn. That's it.

The Upskill or Lay Off Question

Helen Patterson raised something during our conversation that I think every leader reading this book needs to sit with. *"Those difficult situations when someone's role is changing significantly"*, she said. *"Well, do you just let them go and lay them all off? Or do you actually say, "We're going to upskill now."* And then she connected it to mentorship: *"That's where the learning and development and the mentoring comes in. You've invested so much time with this person in your organization. Change is constant. We know that there's going to be something again in a decade."*

This is a HUGE leadership choice point. And it's happening right now, in real time, in organizations everywhere. Some companies are using AI as an excuse to cut headcount. They're attributing layoffs to AI when the real reasons are bad management, over-hiring during the pandemic, or simple cost-cutting that has nothing to do with technology. And the headlines amplify this because *"AI Replaces*

500 Jobs" gets more clicks than *"Company Mismanaged Growth and Downsized".*

The better path, the SMARTER path, is what Helen described. You upskill. You invest in the people you already have. You help them hop. Because here's the business case that doesn't make the news: the cost of replacing an employee is typically 50-200% of their annual salary. The cost of training that same employee in AI skills? A FRACTION of that. And you get to keep all their institutional knowledge, their relationships, their understanding of your business, their judgment.

Laying someone off and "using AI" is almost always going to be more expensive and less effective than training the person you already have to work WITH AI.

What the Real Goal Actually Is

Melissa Penton cuts through all the noise about productivity and efficiency and all the corporate jargon that gets layered onto this conversation with this: *"The real goal is to make room in your life for things that matter to you",* she said. *"Getting rid of all that busy work. Being able to get AI to do something for me so I have time to crochet or do DIY projects or go for hikes with my family. That's more the goal than just being productive."*

And I love this because it reframes the ENTIRE conversation away from "AI replaces your job" toward "AI replaces the WORST PARTS of your job".

The grunt work. The repetitive tasks. The soul-crushing admin that nobody went to school for and nobody is passionate about. All of which leaks into way more than 8 hours a day. THAT is what AI is best at replacing.

Not you. Your busy work.

Melissa talked about how the productivity narrative dominated the early years of generative AI. *"This thing took me an hour, it can take me 15 minutes, so we've saved 45 minutes."* And then the dangerous follow-up reaction (either from yourself or from the powers-that-be): *"Great, now do four times as much work."*

That is the WRONG response. And both Melissa and I feel strongly about this. The right response is: what do you want to do with those 45 minutes that actually matters? Can you spend them in what Gay Hendricks calls your "zone of genius" instead of your zone of mere competence? Can you spend them on strategic thinking instead of data entry? On human connection instead of formatting spreadsheets? On creative problem-solving instead of copy-pasting between systems? On actually working less hours?

Because THAT is where the hope actually lives. Not in doing more. In doing BETTER. In being more human, not less.

Helen Patterson has been saying this from her HR perspective for years: *"How do we use all of these resources and tools and technology to allow the business, the HR professionals, to alleviate all that day to day grunt work so that we can actually help people grow, help people develop and create and be innovative?"*

More space. Not more output.

That's the promise. And it's a promise that's already being kept for the folx who are willing to see it.

Mini Exercise: The Hop Map

Grab a piece of paper. Draw a line down the middle.

On the left side, write your current role, your current skills, and the things you're genuinely good at. Not what your job title says. What you ACTUALLY do well. Are you good at explaining complex things simply? Good at organizing chaos? Good at connecting with people? Good at writing? Good at asking the right questions? Write it all down.

On the right side, write down three AI-adjacent roles that interest you. They don't have to be full career changes. They can be expansions. "My current role + AI governance." "My current role + AI training facilitation." "My current role + AI policy input."

Now draw lines connecting your skills on the left to the roles on the right.

I'm willing to bet you'll find at least two or three connections that surprise you. Skills you already have that are directly applicable to roles that are actively being created and funded.

That's your hop map.

And if you want to take it one step further? Open up whatever AI tool you use and type this: "Here are my current skills: [paste your left column or upload a photo]. What AI-adjacent roles would be a natural extension of these skills, and what would I need to learn to be qualified?"

Let the tool that's "taking your job" help you find your next one. *(If that isn't poetic justice, I don't know what is.)*

This, and all the other mini exercises in this book are in one easy place for you to access. Scan the QR code below or visit: https://wearenorthlightai.com/swan-dive-backwards

CHAPTER 16

The Swan Dive

This book is the proof.

I need to tell you how this book was made.

Not because the behind-the-scenes of writing a book is inherently fascinating *(it's not; it involves a lot of pacing, a lot of voice notes to yourself, and an alarming amount of coffee).*

But because this book was made using the exact process this book describes.

And if I don't tell you that, I've missed the whole point.

The 30-Day Dare

At the end of 2025, Dan Sanchez (Host of AI-driven Marketer and Solo: Scaled) and Ken Freire (co-host of Solo: Scaled) threw down a challenge. Record 30 podcast episodes in 30 days. Turn them into a book. They were doing an experiment and asked anyone who was interested to join.

I don't know if anyone else was crazy enough to accept. I was.

Because I had this book in my head and I wanted to get it out before we turned the calendar. I'd been talking about AI literacy on my podcast for a while. I'd been using this phrase, "swan dive backwards", in conversations, on LinkedIn, at events. People kept asking me, "Are you writing a book?"

Enough times that I noticed.

And so I said yes to the dare. I would record the 30 day daily sprint. Some would be solo teaching episodes where I laid out frameworks. Some would be conversations with guests who are doing remarkable work in the AI space. And then I would take all of that raw material, all 25 transcripts (I ended up publishing 25 episodes in 30 days), all 12 guest voices (and one AIPC case study), all the messy, brilliant, sometimes exhausted recordings, and I would turn them into a book.

Using AI.

(Because of course I'm using AI to help write the book about AI. It would be ridiculous if I didn't.)

Note: Dan and Ken wrote and published their book 'Own the Show'. You can find it at https://ownthe.show

The Name

A few episodes into the sprint, I wrote a post about it on LinkedIn. And something very cool happened.

A name popped up in my comments. Someone from many moons ago. (Or maybe many suns ago, given how much time has passed.) Her name is Alison Garwood-Jones. She was one of my professors when I did my Digital Marketing Strategy certificate at the University of Toronto.

And she wrote this: *"I really hope you get this book done. And I really hope you call it Swan Dive Backwards. I'll leave the subtitle to you."*

When I read that, something just landed.

LANDED.

The book had a name. The energy was right. The story was baked into the title. And I didn't expect my book to be named three or four episodes into a 30-day sprint. But that's what happens when you experiment in public. The universe sends you an Alison Garwood-Jones at exactly the right moment.

The Messy Middle

I want to be honest about this part. Because the whole book has been about being honest, and it would be pretty hypocritical to wrap it all up in a bow and pretend the process was smooth.

It wasn't.

About nine episodes in, twelve days deep, I recorded a solo episode that was basically a coffee chat with the listener. And in it, I said this: *"I'm tired. I'm not necessarily burned out because I'm super energized about this. But it's a lot of talking and thinking and holding of structure in my head."*

I could have skipped that day. I'd already skipped a few. But I showed up anyway. Not because I'm some kind of disciplined hero. Because I wanted to mark the moment. Because I wanted the messy middle to be part of the story.

And here's why that matters for YOU.

If you're in the middle of building AI into your organization, into your workflow, into your career, there WILL be a day where you're tired. Where the momentum has slowed. Where the initial excitement has faded and what's left is just... the work.

That's the messy middle. And the messy middle is where everything good actually gets built. The answer isn't more intensity. It's consistency. Small, honest experiments. One episode at a time. One workflow at a time. One conversation at a time.

Some days I had big idea days. Some days a guest would come on and blow my mind with something I'd never considered. And some days it was just me getting one thing done a few minutes faster because I used AI.

All of those count. ALL of them.

How AI Actually Built This Book

Let me pull back the curtain all the way.

AI was my thinking partner for structure. I would record voice notes, sometimes five-minute rambles, and my LLM of choice would help me turn fuzzy ideas into rough outlines. *"Split this into three parts." "Turn this section into five talking points." "Where does this guest's insight fit into the four pillars?"*

AI was my drafting support. Once I had the outlines, I would build out the chapters, pulling in guest quotes, weaving in frameworks, layering in the voice and personality that you've been reading for the last sixteen chapters. Every chapter went through multiple rounds. AI helped me find the right structure. I made the editorial choices.

AI was my pattern spotter. With 25 transcripts from conversations with 12 different guests as well as one AIPC case study, there was a LOT of raw material. AI helped me see where the themes clustered. Where one guest's insight connected to another's. Where a framework from Episode 259 belonged in the same chapter as a story from Episode 268. That kind of synthesis across dozens of hours of conversation is something that would have taken me months to do alone. AI didn't do it FOR me. It helped me SEE it.

And AI was my energy manager. Helping me draft emails to guests. Organizing my recording schedule. Turning show notes into something publishable. Managing the thousand small tasks that pile up when you're sprinting.

But here's what AI did NOT do.

AI did not decide which guests to invite. I did.

AI did not decide which stories mattered. I did.

AI did not decide when to push back on an idea or when to let a quote breathe. I did.

AI did not decide the voice. The parenthetical whispers. The strategic ALL CAPS. The "folx".

AI did not feel the exhaustion of day twelve, or the thrill of hearing Chris McMartin say *"I don't know any men who apologize for finding ways to do things better"* or the quiet conviction of Helen Patterson talking about One Million Mentor Moments, or the pure fire of Gazzy Amin saying *"what a beautiful time to be a woman".*

A human felt all of that. A human decided it mattered. A human built it into a book.

The tool made me faster.

If that sounds familiar, it should. It's the paintbrush versus photocopier framework from Chapter 12. And this book is the proof that it works.

The Five Moves, One More Time

Way back in Chapter 1, I introduced you to the Five Moves of a Swan Dive. I want to walk through them one more time. This time as the story of this book.

Move One: Spot the Cliff.
I realized that AI was a milestone technology. The kind that changes what normal work looks like. And I realized I had something to say about it. Something specific. Something grounded in real conversations with real people doing real work.

That was my cliff.

Move Two: Check the Water.
I jumped. I spent two years experimenting. Building custom GPTs and Skills. Training clients. Running my AI implementation mastermind. Testing what works and what spectacularly doesn't. I learned to

question the output. I learned where AI is brilliant and where it falls flat on its face.

That was my guardrail step.

Move Three: The Actual Swan Dive.
I said yes to the 30-day challenge. I recorded the episodes. I invited the guests. I showed up on the tired days. I started using AI on REAL work, which is to say, the actual book that needed to exist, not a theoretical exercise.

That was the jump.

(For context, this is my second book. My first book "UNboring: Take your content marketing from blah to brilliant" too me 3 years of actual writing, editing, and publishing. And 10 years before that of thinking about it. For this book, it took me 4 months to write and publish. And only a year before that of thinking about it haha. That's still a quantum collapsing of time. And much greater speed to marketing and learning velocity! I'll take it.)

Move Four: Surface With a Map.
The transcripts became frameworks. The conversations became chapters. The messy experiments became a structured argument for why AI adoption is a literacy problem, not a technology problem. Why culture is the operating system. Why mentorship is infrastructure. Why hope is not naive.

That's was the first draft of this book.

Move Five: Build the Bridge.
A swan dive backwards is not a permanent operating model. The goal is not to keep diving forever. The goal is to build a bridge so that the

next person who comes to this spot on the trail doesn't have to make the same leap of faith.

That's what you're holding. This book is the bridge.

Not because it has all the answers. It doesn't. Nobody does. But because it takes the dive I made and turns it into something you can WALK across.

What I Want You to Take With You

If you've read this far, you've been through a lot with me. Shadow AI and literacy divides. Audits and flywheels. Champions and bridge builders. Creativity frameworks and ROI that goes beyond time saved. The gender gap. 35,000 reasons for hope.

And now this. The story behind the story.

Here is what I want you to carry out of this book and into your Monday morning.

You don't need to be an expert. Nobody is. The people who are furthest ahead are just the ones who started earliest and asked the most questions. Eventually we'll all be in the same place and this thing will run in the background like the internet.

You don't need a perfect plan. You need a next step. One workflow. One conversation. One "let me try this and see what happens". One hop.

You don't need more tools. The AI will keep getting better, faster, cheaper. Feel no FOMO.

You don't need to be brave. You need to be willing. Willing to start before you're ready. Willing to be a beginner. Willing to say "I don't know" and have that be okay. Willing to show up on the tired days.

And you absolutely, positively, do not need permission.

You never did.

A moment of gratitude

The Voices in This Book

You know at this point that this book was built from 25 podcast episodes recorded over 30 days. Thirteen of those were solo teaching episodes where I laid out frameworks, shared stories, and talked to myself more than any reasonable human should. The other episodes were conversations with twelve remarkable humans who said yes during the busiest month of the year (December 2025).

Every one of them brought something I couldn't have written on my own. Their stories, their expertise, their willingness to be honest on the record about what's actually happening with AI in the real world. These are the voices you've been reading throughout this book.

Here they are.

Gazzy Amin Founder, Sales Beyond Scripts

Gazzy is the kind of entrepreneur who makes you want to get off the couch and go build something. She runs Sales Beyond Scripts, where she helps entrepreneurs scale through sales strategy, coaching, and

CEO-level business planning. She showed up to our conversation with the energy of someone who uses AI in her actual life every single day, from writing Facebook ad scripts with ChatGPT to running full-day business planning intensives where AI is woven into the coaching process. Her line, *"What a beautiful time to be a woman"*, became one of the emotional anchors of this book.

Instagram: https://www.instagram.com/authenticgazzy

Website: authenticgazzy.com

Shona Boyd Product Manager | AI Approachability Advocate

Shona is a product manager in the SaaS space who made a conscious decision to be visible in AI when she noticed that not a lot of people who looked like her were leading the conversation. She came to AI through a real problem (figuring out what job seekers actually wanted when they wouldn't get interviews) and stayed because she saw the gap between who was talking about AI and who needed to hear about it. Her commitment to making this technology approachable for people who might otherwise feel like it isn't for them runs through the belonging thread of this book.

LinkedIn: https://www.linkedin.com/in/lashonaboyd

Heather Cannings Women's Entrepreneurship Program Lead, Nventure | StrikeUp Conference

Heather is the force behind StrikeUp, a free digital conference for women entrepreneurs that draws thousands from across Canada and beyond. Through Nventure, she works directly with women business owners navigating growth, funding, and now AI adoption. She brought the data that reframed my entire understanding of the gender gap in

AI: the 11pm learning sessions, the "cheating" feelings, the systemic barriers that statistics alone don't capture. Her perspective on building support systems that meet women where they actually ARE (on mobile, on lunch breaks, in stolen moments) shaped some of the most important arguments in this book.

LinkedIn: linkedin.com/in/heathercannings

Website: strikeup.ca

Jason Dea Go-to-Market & Product Management, Coru Ventures

Jason works at a Toronto-based venture studio focused on zero-to-one innovation, and he brought a rare perspective to our conversation: that of someone who lives inside the startup and SaaS world where AI isn't theoretical. It's the job. He's the one who broke down how to turn messy experiments into repeatable workflows, and who described building a team of specialized mini-AIs (bumblebees), each trained for a specific micro-task, rather than trying to make one tool do everything. His approach to AI as a series of hyper-specific collaborators makes so much practical sense.

LinkedIn: linkedin.com/in/jasondea

Website: jasondea.com

Suzanne Huber Go-to-Market Consultant

Suzanne is my business buddy, my co-working partner, and one of the wisest people I know. She's a go-to-market consultant and a writer who has been using AI since 2022 to enrich her work and her clients' work. Our episode together was a masterclass in how expertise still matters in the age of AI: the machine gives you a first draft, but your critical thinking, your taste, and your point of view are what make it worth reading. Her sister's framing of 'robot arms' that Suzanne brought to our discussion is one of those things that takes so much of the fear around AI off the table.

LinkedIn: linkedin.com/in/suzanneleehuber

Website: suzanne-huber.medium.com

Jennifer Hufnagel AI Readiness Consultant & Educator, Hufnagel Consulting

Jennifer and I met in the most elite way possible: we were both quoted in the Globe and Mail talking about women and AI. She's an educator at her core, with a background in business analysis, digital adoption, and learning and development. She pivoted fully into AI readiness when clients started asking her to build AI training workshops. She's the one who told me, flat out, that she doesn't build e-learning because she doesn't believe you can learn AI through online courses. Her framing of the "guide on the side" versus the "sage on the stage" and her insistence on communities of practice are some of my favourite parts of our interview.

LinkedIn: linkedin.com/in/jennifer-hufnagel

Website: hufnagelconsulting.ca

Andrew Jenkins Founder, Volterra Digital | Author, Social Media Marketing for Business | Former University of Toronto Instructor

Andrew was my teacher before he was my guest. He taught social media strategy at the University of Toronto, which is where I did my Digital Marketing Strategy certificate. He leads Volterra Digital, an international social media agency based in Toronto, and hosts The Low Production High Value Show podcast. Andrew's contribution to this book is deeply personal to me because he represents the full-circle nature of learning. His approach to having the machine talk to itself opens up entirely new ways of thinking about AI for the readers of this book.

LinkedIn: linkedin.com/in/andrewjjenkins

Website: volterradigital.com

Dr. Jim Kanichirayil Founder, Cascading Leadership

Dr. Jim runs Cascading Leadership, a go-to-market agency for early-stage founders. He partners with founders on a fractional basis to get them from zero to product-market fit. He opens conversations with a Dr. Evil impression, which tells you everything you need to know about his energy. His contributions to our multi-guest episode brought the founder's lens to the AI conversation: how to think about build-versus-buy decisions, how to evaluate tools when you're resource-constrained, and how to make AI work when you're a small team.

LinkedIn: linkedin.com/in/drjimk

Website: https://www.cascadingleadership.com

Chris McMartin National Lead, Scotiabank Women Initiative for Business Banking | Co-host, I Am Unbreakable Podcast

Chris does not sugarcoat. She is the Business Banking National Lead for Scotiabank Women Initiative, which means she has a front-row seat to how women entrepreneurs are actually engaging with AI in their businesses. She came on the podcast and said things that stopped me cold: that women are using AI at a fraction of its capability because they're afraid to ask questions, that the grants are there but women aren't applying because they assume "that's not for me", and the line I haven't been able to stop thinking about since she said it: "I don't know any men who apologize for finding ways to do things better."

LinkedIn: linkedin.com/in/chris-mcmartin

Website: https://www.scotiabank.com/women-initiative/ca/en.html

Leigh Mitchell Chief ChangeMaker, Women in Biz Network | Host, ChangeMaker Leader Podcast | Professor, York University SCS & University of Guelph-Humber

Leigh is a member of AI Power Circle and a key person who's proved, in real time, what happens when community meets curiosity. She came in experimenting. And in quantum timelines, she was building websites, training others, and holding space for deep conversations on AI ethics across her wide network of women entrepreneurs. She's also the kind of person who raises her hand and says "I want to be part of this" - whether it's AI literacy efforts, events, or helping someone - which is exactly the energy this book is about.

LinkedIn: linkedin.com/in/mitchellleigh

Website: womeninbiznetwork.com

Helen Patterson Founder, Life Works Well | Author, Create a Mentor Culture | One Million Mentor Moments Initiative

Helen is a senior human resources leader with decades of experience spanning HR, legal, and organizational culture. She runs Life Works Well, consults on heart-centered culture for scaling businesses, is the author of Create a Mentor Culture, and the creator of One Million Mentor Moments. She reminds us that mentoring is powerful infrastructure for AI adoption. She brought 25 years of perspective to a three-year-old technology and made it make sense.

LinkedIn: linkedin.com/in/lifeworkswell

Website: lifeworkswell.ca

Melissa Penton Change Manager & AI Lead, Sun Life | Writer, Confessions of an AI User (Substack)

Melissa calls herself a "purple person", someone who sits between the tech world and the business world and translates between the two. She's a change manager by career, now leading AI initiatives at Sun Life, and she writes about her journey on Substack with the kind of honesty that makes you feel like you're not alone in figuring this out. She's the one who reframed the entire productivity narrative for me: the goal isn't to do more, it's to make room in your life for things that actually matter. She joined us from Dublin, Ireland, proving that you AI collaboration spans borders and oceans.

LinkedIn: linkedin.com/in/melissadpenton

Substack: confessionsofanaiuser.substack.com

Kirsten Schmidtke Sales Coach and Consultant

Kirsten works at the intersection of mindset and skillset in sales and sales leadership. We met at a business event where she was speaking, and the conversation that followed convinced me she had to be part of this book. She brought the language of scale to the AI conversation: how do we do more with less, reduce effort to create more impact, and stop confusing output with outcome. Her reminder that AI "is not here to replace us, it's giving us space to be even better versions of ourselves" is one of those lines that sounds simple until you sit with it.

LinkedIn: linkedin.com/in/kirstenschmidtke

Website: kirstenschmidtke.com

Voices Behind This Book

The guests you've met throughout these chapters are the voices IN this book. But there are voices BEHIND it. People who didn't appear on the podcast but without whom none of this would exist.

My husband, Mithran Stone, held down every single thing that needed holding while I recorded 25 episodes in 30 days during the busiest month of the year. He didn't complain. He made dinner. He kept our life running while I was locked in my office talking to a microphone. He's also the Bridge Builder in our household, which means he's the reason any of my wild ideas ever become actual infrastructure. I swan dive. He builds the bridge. We work.

My teen is the reason I care so much about the future of AI literacy. Everything I build, every framework I teach, every conversation I have about closing the gap, is because I want the world this kid inherits to be one where the tools are accessible, the opportunities are equitable, and the humans are still in charge.

My mom has been my biggest cheerleader since before I knew what cheerleading was. She's the kind of mother who will read every word of this book, even the parts she doesn't fully understand, and then tell everyone she knows about it. That kind of unconditional belief in another human is rare. I got lucky.

Arun Diaz, my uncle, was the first person who said, "You need to write an AI book." He looked at the work I was doing in the trenches from the very start of generative AI and said: write the book. So. Here's the book!

Alison Garwood-Jones named this book in a LinkedIn comment. She was my professor at the University of Toronto years ago, and when she wrote "I really hope you call it Swan Dive Backwards", the whole project snapped into focus. Some people change the trajectory of a thing in one sentence. Alison is one of those people.

LinkedIn: linkedin.com/in/alisongarwoodjones

Website: alisongarwoodjones.com

Dan Sanchez and Ken Freire are the reason this book exists as a 4-month reality and not a "someday" project. They created the 30-day podcast-to-book challenge that I was either brave or unhinged enough to accept. Their generosity in sharing the process, the framework, and the challenge itself gave me the structure to turn an idea into a book. If you're sitting on a book and you need someone to shove you off the cliff (lovingly, with a map), these are your people.

Dan Sanchez LinkedIn: linkedin.com/in/digitalmarketingdan

Ken Freire LinkedIn: linkedin.com/in/kenfreire

Their book website: ownthe.show

The members of AI Power Circle, my AI implementation mastermind, were the live laboratory for half the frameworks in this book. They were testing the flywheel. They were running audits. They showed up on Wednesdays, they did the work, and they gave me real-time proof that this stuff actually lands when real humans try it in real businesses. You know who you are. Thank you for being the proof.

The listeners of AI Literacy for Entrepreneurs who followed along during the 30-day sprint in real time. You left ratings. You sent DMs. You shared episodes with people who needed to hear them. You were the first audience for the raw, sometimes messy, sometimes tired material that eventually became the book you're holding. This started as a podcast for you. It became a book because of you.

Made in United States
North Haven, CT
04 November 2026

21764039R00150